Prepare My Prayer
Recipes to Awaken the Soul

Makor Chaim Institutions
Gush Etzion

MAGGID

Dov Singer

Prepare My Prayer
RECIPES TO AWAKEN THE SOUL

Edited and adapted by Reut Brosh
Translated by Leah Hartman

Makor Chaim
Maggid Books

Prepare My Prayer
Recipes to Awaken the Soul

First English Edition, 2020

Maggid Books
An imprint of Koren Publishers Jerusalem Ltd.

POB 8531, New Milford, CT 06776-8531, USA
& POB 4044, Jerusalem 9104001, Israel
www.korenpub.com

Original Hebrew Edition © Dov Singer, 2017
English Translation © Dov Singer, 2020

Cover and design: Eliyahu Misgav and "Cursive Aleph-Bet"
Calligraphy by Izzy Pludwinski

The publication of this book was made possible
through the generous support of *Torah Education in Israel*.

All rights reserved. No part of this publication may be reproduced,
stored in a retrieval system, or transmitted in any form or by
any means, electronic, mechanical, photocopying, or otherwise,
without the prior permission of the publisher, except in the case
of brief quotations embedded in critical articles or reviews.

ISBN 978-1-59264-537-4, *hardcover*

A CIP catalogue record for this title is
available from the British Library

Printed and bound in the United States

"יה זכות אבות יגן עלינו"

ספר זה מוקדש
לעילוי נשמת הורינו האהובים
יוסף מאיר וצפורה גליק ז"ל
עקיבא הולנדר ז"ל

ולכבודה של
אסתר הולנדר תבדל"א

ולעילוי נשמת אחיי
אלכסנדר וטיבי גליק הי"ד
שנספו בשואה

ולעילוי נשמת דודי
יוסף הולנדר הי"ד
שנפל במלחמת השחרור

In loving memory and

לעילוי נשמת
ר' יואל זאב בן ר' יוסף הלוי ז"ל
כ"ז שבט ה'תשס"ח

"בגלל אבות תושיע בנים ותביא גאולה לבני בניהם"

In Loving Memory of
Rabbi I. Fred Hollander *z"l*
Rabbi David & Faye Hollander *z"l*

🕊 🕊

"כי עמך מקור חיים באורך נראה אור"

*Dedicated in honor of the staff,
students, and alumni of Makor Chaim
and in memory of our students and alumni
who died sanctifying G-d's name*

Contents

A Journey to the Land of Prayer *by Elhanan Nir* xv
Translator's Preface xxiii
At the Gate xxvii

Let Me Enter Your House
Opening: Let Us Enter Your Gates 4
Opening the Senses 6
Running to Prayer 8
May It Be Your Desire 10
Finding Favor 14
All the Way In 16

Know Before Whom You Stand
Opening: Standing Present 24
Perceiving the Presence 26
I, You, and He 30
Calling by Name 34
Prayer as Standing in Judgment 36
Silence 38

Soul Movements in Prayer

Opening: Song of the Heart 44

Giving Thanks 46

Praise 50

Supplications 54

Yearnings 56

Crying Out 60

The Prayers of Our Forefathers 64

    Standing for Himself: Abraham 66

    Conversation: Isaac 68

    Up Against the Wall: Jacob 70

Don't Be Stubborn 72

A Melody 74

Call of the Heart 76

The Body's Gestures

Opening: Wordless 82

Standing 84

Bowing 88

Falling 90

Our Hands in Prayer 92

Breathing 94

Sighing 96

Speaking to the Body 98

Fixed Prayer and Pleading

Opening: Renewal in Prayer 104
From Mumbling to Facing 106
Elevating the Worlds 110
The Daily Prayer 114
Making It New..116
Prayer as Supplication 118
A Little Bit Is Good 124

Communal Prayer

Opening: Praying as One..130
Prayer Through the Generations 132
Love Your Friend as Yourself..134
The Community's Prayer...136
Sheliaḥ Tzibur, an Emissary of Prayer 138
The Prayer of the Collective 140
Prayer for the *Shekhina*...144
Advice for Praying in Community 146

Prayers of Ancient Days

Opening: Inheritance of Our Ancestors 152
A Short Prayer..154
I Have Become Small...156
The One Who Answered Will Answer Us......................160

Hezekiah's Prayer ... 164
Psalms ... 166

Listening for a Response
Opening: Face to Face ... 174
An Answer in Words ... 176
The Priestly Blessing ... 180
Torah Reading, Calling ... 182
Hearing Is Responding ... 186

Disturbances in Prayer
Opening: Service of the Heart ... 192
Raising Up Stray Thoughts ... 194
Penetrating the Barrier ... 196
Shine Light on the Word ... 200
Praying Through the *Tzaddik* ... 204
God Praying ... 206

Hitbodedut: Private Prayer from the Heart
Opening: Alone ... 212
The Initial Step of *Hitbodedut* ... 214
Praying in the Field ... 218
Requesting in *Hitbodedut* ... 222
Hitbodedut: A Sharing ... 224
Drawing Out Prayers ... 226
One Who Prays for a Friend ... 228

In Constant Conversation

Opening: Be a Master of Prayer!	236
Have You Looked at the Skies Today?	238
Hints	240
Writing Prayers	242
In Closing, a Prayer	246
Copyright list	248
About the Author	251

A Journey to the Land of Prayer

Elhanan Nir

Rabbi Dov Singer suggests that we view prayer as a part of the entirety of the modern human condition. Restoring one's relationship with oneself and one's environment is the gateway to the face-to-face encounter with the Divine.

The Essence of the Encounter

Rabbi Dov Singer is the first student of a trio of rabbis who heralded the Hasidic revival in Israel's National-Religious community in the late twentieth century. The three rabbis – Rabbi Shagar *z"l*, Rabbi Menachem Froman *z"l*, and Rabbi Adin Steinsaltz – are responsible for the change of the discourse of this community. While the National-Religious community lives according to a collective language and ideology, these three teachers sought to suggest a religious language that is gentler, more personal, a language that leaves room for dialogue. In place of exclamation points (to which great ideologues are often partial), these three rabbis, each in his own way, cultivated a more particular, more subjective language – a language that allows space for questions marks, for grappling, and draws from the awareness that life here is ever hazy and in constant search of the hidden presence, of holiness. And instead of pious and all-knowing answers, the three spiritual teachers legitimized existential questions: who am I? What do I want to do here? And mainly – what is the purpose and the goal of this world? They recognized in these questions the opening to a meeting place with the Beyond, with the Infinite.

The student, Rabbi Singer, also emphasized these points. He wrote: "When a person meets a riddle – it will remain with him his whole life. But if he meets only an answer – when he grows up, it will seem to him childish and irrelevant." But, like his rabbis, he did not content himself with engaging with Hasidic content; he found ways to work with form and to build a contemporary, concrete toolbox whose purpose is to bring about this inner space of searching and dialogue.

Rabbi Dov Singer began his path as the head of the Makor Chaim Yeshiva High School, located in Gush Etzion, over three decades ago, a position he holds to this day. At the yeshiva, which was founded by Rabbi Steinsaltz, he developed a number of foundational principles which he would continue to strengthen in the years to come:

1. Trust: the main role of the educator is to grow, nourish, and work towards a sense of trust and faith.
2. Wholeness: in an atmosphere of trust, one does not have to put on a false display of perfection, but rather to accept the other where he is. The teacher is not a perfect person, a genius or a *tzaddik* [righteous person], but rather a believer who knows how to project his faith to the student and to others. He learns just as he teaches. The more years a person studies, the more

he becomes a student, and the less he knows. This inner stance cultivates humanistic values of dignity and compassion for all human existence, arising out of a religious value of standing in the presence of God.

3. Speaking and Listening: speaking correctly and honestly between two, as well as listening truthfully between two, is the gateway not only to human relationships but also to the relationship between humans and God. Speaking and listening are the gateway to every relationship – between spouses, friends, parents and children, and also the relationship between humans and God. This is the gateway to prayer.

4. Presence: People must be fully present in reality, must make space for others to be present in reality, and must make room for the hidden presence, for God, and be present with them.

In later years, Rabbi Dov established the *Beit Midrash LeHithadshut* (The Study Center for Renewal), a center of Torah study for working people, where he sought to study and to teach the foundations laid out here. It includes two major programs: First, *Lifnai VeLifnim* is a teacher training program that provides tools for educators to do their own inner work, with the understanding that the only possibility a teacher has of encouraging growth in students, and of building a proper relationship with them, is through the constant learning and renewal of the teacher. *Lifnai VeLifnim* is a program available to Israeli college and university students as a part of their undergraduate and graduate studies, which makes this unique method accessible to students across Israel. In recent years, together with the Orthodox Union and friends from around the Jewish world, the *Beit Midrash LeHithadshut* has shared this method in various forms with communities and schools from numerous countries.

The second program is the *Az Nidberu* prayer groups: groups of people who meet once a week for two or three hours and discuss their lives, their spiritual work, that which is truly important – a sharing that is open, personal, and genuine. In contrast to the psychoanalytic method, which asks people to turn inward into themselves, to dig and dig into their past, seeking to reach an inner catharsis, these prayer groups take people outside of themselves. They ask one to connect to a context broader than one's own existence: a context of family and friends, of community and nation, and even of the world, and this very connection begins the flow of prayer. This book was born out of these prayer groups, and it is an invitation to all – men and women, Jews and non-Jews alike – to initiate such groups whose purpose is to learn to speak, to listen, and to pray.

A Renewed Encounter with Prayer

Rabbi Dov came to his involvement with prayer through his work with couples who were experiencing marital difficulties. They would come to him to learn how to talk and to listen, to enhance their marital connection, and to improve the language of communication between them. After many conversations with couples he realized that the marital tools that can facilitate communication between and husband and wife are actually the same tools that can open the gates of prayer, and since then he has worked hard to revive and encourage prayer. Most people have never experienced a conversation in which they have felt truly heard. They do not have the inner experience of their words reaching their destination. A person who is unfamiliar with this element of listening, even if he is a person of deep faith, does not know how to pray, for this person does not know what it means to really hear. Therefore, before we prove God's existence, we must make the Creator, the Beyond, the Universe in which we live, present. This is done through prayer.

The Mishna in *Avot* tells us that the world is based on three pillars: Torah, prayer, and acts of kindness. The world of Torah learning deals with the realm of Torah, the social world with the realm of acts of kindness, but no one touches the realm of prayer. Prayer is in a deep freeze: no one approaches it, no one touches it, no one engages with it. But removing it from the freezer is our chance, as humans. Prayer is the prospect of a person's salvation from being firmly absorbed in him- or herself, from the fences of loneliness with which people surround their lives. It is the way to the freedom every human deserves. Prayer is therefore the vision of the liberation of the modern man from his inner shackles, the liberation of the person wherever he is. One can speak about prayer, or one can just pray. The willingness to enter into that experience is the opportunity to consider theological questions and to talk about God, but it does not work the other way around – you cannot talk about God without ever having a true experience of prayer.

According to Rabbi Dov, the difficulty of praying lies not necessarily in the technological environment that surrounds us, but rather in something far more fundamental – the difficulty we humans have with being weak, being in a position of requesting, of submission and giving in, of seeking help. To pray is to learn to speak, to listen, and to be weak. Prayer demands of me to bring my life to a place beyond myself, to convert it from the 'I-It' to the 'I-Thou' and the 'Eternal Thou,' to use Martin Buber's well-known concepts. This is a redemptive vision where humans are released from their inner cage, where they arise from broken and superficial relationships with themselves and their environment and emerge to be reflected on the shore of prayer, where they learn to reach out and meet the other.

One of the main problems with prayer is that most people have not ever experienced true listening. Most of us have never felt heard, and we have never really heard others. If a person has merited to be truly attentive, he has a way of facing the Ultimate Listener. He knows his words are heard. The problem of communication is not a lack of concentration, but a lack of trust in the words. Words have ceased to be words that emerge from the heart and return to it, but have become merely a means of sharing information. They no longer carry within them the emotion and the soul, as they are supposed to. They must be redeemed, the trust in the words restored, to lead us to a consciousness where when I say "Good morning" my words are the blessing they are truly meant to be, rather than a hollow, dry expression, empty and lifeless. When one learns to speak, to listen, and to make space, he develops an ability to enter into a situation where sharing is made possible; he learns to stand before God and feel his ability to be someone who is heard.

You sit with a friend, looking closely at him or her and trying to experience – really experience – that there is someone here. You look deeply, noticing your friend's presence. And now you say to your friend the most precious word in the world: "You." This is the peak of prayer – the created man says to the Creator: "You."

From the moment that there is "you," there is "he," but the "he" is other. Most people tend to see the other as something, as a function of this or that, and not as someone. In order to distinguish the other as someone and not merely something, I must first make space to meet this other as a someone, as a wonder. Inside this human creation, someone, not just something, is moving about, and when I learn to meet that someone, I learn that everything is personal. It is not an idea, it is a feeling of presence. Life itself.

Indeed, prayer is often difficult for us – we feel we are speaking but there is no answer; we speak for years and years, but there is no echo to our words or our cries. Truly, this is a debilitating condition and can even lead to despair. But it requires one to remain open to an answer that is different from what one may have expected: the ability to verbalize the secrets of the heart – this is the real answer of prayer. "A man may arrange his thoughts, but what he says depends on God" (Prov. 16:1). The very act of speech is God's answer to humans turning towards Him, calling to Him from our place. The speech itself also functions as proof of the existence of God. But this is not an external proof of the existence of God; rather, it is a willingness to enter into the inside. This "inside" is itself the Divine Presence in the world, the understanding that in truth I am not alone here in the world, even if it is a world seemingly full of alienation and strangeness.

And what about when we have challenges with the Creator, there is resentment in the heart, the soul is constrained and refuses to continue trusting? If it is arbitrary it is one thing, but if one perceives that there are complexities and difficulties in the world, it is another, says Rabbi Dov. I do not understand what is happening, but I understand that something is happening here, that it is not injustice but a kind of calling to me that I must learn even though I may never understand. I surrender understanding and prefer to simply meet, just as I do not try to explain the other, but prefer to remain opposite and discover his or her presence.

This book is a journey to the unknown land of prayer, but no less to the land of listening and speaking, to the land of presence with the other and with the hiddenness of life, to the land of encounter. It has many trails, polar geographies and varying climates, mountains and rivers, heights and depths, streams of water and arid deserts, and each and every time a person can choose their own route. And like any good trip – one never knows what the road will bring, what will happen there and how it will end.

Because the journey is the secret of this life, here.

Rabbi Elhanan Nir teaches at the Siach Yitzchak and Machanayim yeshivas in Gush Etzion and is the editor of the "Musaf Shabbat" culture supplement of the Makor Rishon newspaper. He has written several celebrated volumes of poetry, two works of Jewish thought, and a novel, and has been awarded the Prime Minister's Prize for Hebrew Literary Works, the Minister of Education's Award for Jewish Culture, and the International Posen Scholarship.

Translator's Preface

Every Hebrew-language text, whether holy or secular, is written in the language of the Jewish Bible and Jewish prayer book. By simply engaging a Hebrew text, the reader – believer or atheist, Jewish or not – is swimming in the inherent richness of the Hebrew word that at every turn calls upon roots soaked with ancient meaning.

Even in the original Hebrew, *Prepare My Prayer* is in and of itself a kind of translation. It is a book that takes the age-old words and movements of the traditional Jewish prayer service and attempts to "carry them over" – the original meaning of the word "translate" – to the modern worshipper. As the author writes: "The written prayer is a fixed prayer / We must make it new / To bring the ancient words inside… / To reveal the movement from which the words were born / Before they were expressed, before they were written."

This book is about words: about how we say them, how we hear them, and how they are heard. It is thus a radical step to take the actual words of the book and translate them into a new language. Jewish tradition teaches that the world was created through a word. Anyone familiar with the Hebrew language knows that each Hebrew word holds worlds within it.

To give the reader a small sense of how this expresses itself in this book, I will share the discussion that surrounded a deceptively simple word: *toda*. It seemed easy enough at first. In English this one word translates into two: "Thank you." When I told this to the author (at his request – it would never have occurred to me to ask), he was taken aback: "Is there really no way to say '*toda*' without using the word 'you'?" I explained that while it is possible to say "thanks," this would be unsuitable, for its casual register lacks real expression of gratitude. Rabbi Singer went on for at least ten minutes about how astounded he was by this idea, and frankly, for a while I didn't get it. Until I did: in the Hebrew, Rabbi Singer insisted, the fact that one says only "*toda*," a word of thanksgiving not specifically addressed to anyone, leaves open the space for the gratitude being expressed to go beyond the specific individual being addressed, to include more than one, including the One.

It may take a teacher of Rabbi Singer's caliber to unlock such meaning for us, but it is right there in the language. This book is full of such carry-overs – some of which worked elegantly, some of which less so. As the book's translator I could spend pages discussing this, but I trust that the reader, while knowing that something is being lost, will nevertheless reap the joy of being to learn from this very important book.

One final point I feel is important to share: the use of gender in language. How this was done in this book was the subject of much discussion between myself and the author, and ultimately we decided that in the sections of the book that are Rabbi Singer's own words, we would attempt, whenever possible, to refrain from gendered language, both attempting to avoid the use of the masculine "he" to refer to both genders, and also in the use of God language.

However, this book is also composed of the writings of others. In every instance where the words are not the author's, i.e., quotes from original sources as well as poetry, we chose to remain as close to possible to the original text, and therefore used gendered language without inhibition. Something is gained when attempting to remove references to gender, but, as in translation, something is lost as well, and we felt this was the most honest and correct way to deal with this.

My own prayer is that the words of this English version will move readers to use their words more openly, and more intently, when speaking to the important people in their lives, and even more so in speaking to God, and will be moved to come a step closer to engaging with Jewish texts in their original.

At the Gate

Service of the Heart

Prayer is the service of the heart. "'And you should serve God with all your heart' (Deut. 11:13). What is the service of the heart? Say it is prayer" (Taanit 2a). The heart is the epicenter of all that happens and the way in which we serve God. This book attempts to offer a language for working with prayer not in the form of study whose content is prayer, but rather through the language of service, the language of the heart: to put our heart into our soul, to give the soul words, and to offer ways we may reach it.

Prayer encompasses our whole being: It peeks out at us from an obtuse day-to-day life at moments of crisis, when a crack appears in the sense of security that envelops us. It smiles at us at moments of great joy. It whispers to us when we are stirred by the beauty of nature or the perfection of a passing moment. The call to prayer is a call to life, a call to open to the deep, primal voice that stirs within us and in all of reality in every moment.

Prayer's great message is the very belief in the power of the desires and the yearnings that beat within us to influence our lives. The power of words, which are the tools with which we express our desire, can change reality. Many people walk about the world believing reality is closed and stuck, and almost impossible to change. Some believe in the power of deeds to fix the world, others choose to look at reality and complain. The one who prays believes in the power of prayer, of words, to soften reality and to forge openings in it. People who pray are like viewers standing in front of a television screen seeing reality through it, when suddenly they discover that the screen is a touch screen, and it is possible to influence what they are watching. One who has experienced reality in this way changes from a guest or an observer to a household member, a partner. Through words it is possible to give freedom to thoughts, to desires and yearnings, and these words penetrate through the screen to their destination.

The first step toward prayer is working on our ability to speak; to speak to one another. "Then the God-fearing men spoke to one another, and the Lord listened and heard it" (Mal. 3:16). It is the training of our ability to be in a meeting place where the speech is born of the connection; the words arise and grow from the meeting of two. In this meeting a friend is not only a screen on which to shine our words, repeating ourselves with the same words we always say, but rather through our meeting, from the essence of our shared presence, something happens. This kind of speech is unique in its existence, words are born. If we were to speak with someone else, the words that would rise between us would be completely different. The new words, bubbling up, become a kind of testing ground for the quality of the meeting. This kind of conversation comes into being through my ability to turn to another with all of myself, to speak in the first person and with words that come from the heart. Beyond the words there is of course the listening: Is our voice heard? Has it reached its destination? Have we heard our friend's voice? Like when a pebble is tossed into a well, our ear is eager to hear it hit the water.

And sometimes a couple, or two good friends, sit and speak heart to heart, and they merit to feel that their words not only reached their hearts, but also touched eternity. Something happened between them that went beyond them. "And God heard and listened." Their words merited to be heard by God. Even though they were not aimed at God, God listened and heard. It's as if they could feel God standing behind the wall, peeking in and listening. The words transformed into prayer, the root of the soul awakened. There was a secret presence between them that gave the speech born amongst them a three-dimensional quality.

When we are able to open our hearts to each other, to speak to each other with real words, with words of closeness, we can direct that same quality of speech to our words with God in prayer, as one speaks to a friend.

These thoughts led me to encourage groups all over Israel to form *ḥavurot* (workshop-style study groups) whose purpose is to come together to seek this heart-to-heart talk in learning, work, and prayer. This kind of direct, personal conversation affects the character of the learning and transforms the learning into a dialogue, which then transforms into prayer. Many of the understandings embedded in this book and the "recipes" which appear in it were born out of the work I did with different *ḥavurot* of prayer.[1]

The Naturalness of Prayer

Many thinkers have given different answers to the philosophical question, which to a great extent is also an existential question for the human race: what is humankind? The best-known answer is the Latin term "*Homo sapiens*," which means a thinking being, or a conscious being. Perhaps we can offer another answer. The human is "*Homo mitpalelos*" (*mitpalel* meaning praying), so a praying being, or, more accurately, a being who, before beginning to pray, yearns. This unique ability of the human soul, to express prayer from within, defines the uniqueness of humans over animals even more distinctly than their ability to think. The expression *maveh*, which appears in the Mishna (Bava Kamma 2a) in reference to humans, is explained in the Talmud (Bava Kamma 3b) to mean a person of will, a person of prayer. There is a constant call, a longing inside people, that whispers to them in waves of ebb and flow. Pleas, desires, requests, words of gratitude. Many times in a person's life, consciously or not, we stand before. Asking for our lives. Yearning. Desiring.

The whole of existence simmers in each moment with underground, wordless voices. It has an underlying will, a hidden prayer. Prayer is an expression of the conversation of

---

[1] As a result of the different prayer groups dispersed throughout Israel, "HaShaar" (The Gate) – A Meeting Place for Service of the Heart – was born. To read more about the activities of HaShaar and the prayer groups, visit the website of the Study Center for Renewal, www.lifnim.co.il.

existence, it brings together a person's deepest desires and the desires concealed in all of existence, and gives words to the prayer of the world, the prayer of humankind.

When I propose to define us, people, as praying beings, I am attempting to free ourselves from the need to explain to ourselves what prayer is, who God is, or whether prayer helps or not. Many times the greatest block to prayer is a theological, intellectual block, which attempts to investigate and understand exactly how it all works. Prayer suggests bypassing these questions and letting them go for a while, in the spirit of "We will do and we will listen" (Ex. 24:7), allowing the naturalness of prayer to work on us, much like the way we breathe, even without understanding completely how the breathing mechanism works.

The human being is not only a creature who yearns, but also one who prays. Hidden in us is the ability not only to be a vessel to receive the spontaneous call of prayer, but also to pray, meaning: to call the prayer to ourselves, to have a relationship with it, to turn it into a state of consciousness that is deliberate and perfected. One of the most meaningful challenges I have merited to meet in my long years as an educator has been teaching about prayer. Despite the accumulation of knowledge of many generations who have studied the prayer book, the different experiences of prayer, and the different forms and meanings that prayer can take on, many times prayer itself eludes us. At times it seems that precisely the abundant possibilities of learning materials about prayer tie our hands, overwhelming the individual seed attempting to grow in its own way. Because of this I am convinced that the best way to teach prayer is to for us to become people who pray. To awaken within ourselves a call to pray, to make space for the service of the heart, for the pray-er inside of us. Not to invent something new, out of nothing, but to open up a movement that has existed inside of us since birth.

The main purpose of the book is to expand the idea of prayer beyond the known boundaries of the synagogue and the prayer book, and to look at the different faces of prayer and its reflections in reality. To awaken the inner spring from which prayer flows and to rejuvenate the words printed in the prayer book. To revive the set prayers, and to discover the prayers that are not printed in the prayer book. To recognize prayer as a kind of state of being, of presence, in which a praying person stands before that which is Presence itself, and strengthens the awareness of the beating heart of the world.

The book is structured like a recipe book – recipes for prayer. Just as the ability to cook and eat is a natural ability and a basic human need, so too prayer is natural, and every person knows deep inside what prayer is. But sometimes it seems that prayer is a language forgotten. This book offers initial models that can help us remember again the forgotten language, exercise our ability to use it, and remind the soul that it is a praying being. Out of trust in the innate naturalness of prayer for people, this book is written as "a little bit that holds a lot." It does not overbear with words and explanations, but comes to gently shake the dust off the wheels of prayer.

When two people prepare a dish using the same recipe, each one will create a different dish, each one with their own fingerprint, their own unique flavors. In a similar way, the use of this book is personal and will take each reader to a different place. The recipe is only a platform from which to begin, and everyone is welcome to play with its raw materials, to experiment and change them as their heart desires. My hope is that through the exercises and experiments, readers will find even more new recipes and configurations in the world of prayer.

Working with this book does not require previous knowledge, but only a willingness to try. Through experimenting with the different textures and tastes of prayer, the experience of prayer will expand. It is possible that in the beginning, some of the recipes will be embarrassing or unsuccessful – it is important not to be deterred by the confusion or difficulty, but rather to dare to keep trying. Many pans were scorched and cookies burnt before reaching the plate…

It is recommended to relate to using this book like the exercising of a muscle – the longer it has not been used, the more likely the possibility of initial pain when stretching it. But soon enough the new movement will become natural and recognized. It is highly recommended to find partners for the work with the recipes of the book – many of them are fitting for a couple, learning partners, or a group. Some of the recipes are intended for communal prayer in the synagogue, while others are for personal prayer times – in a quiet room at home, in the garden, or another beloved location. For best results, it is better to make time and remove all distractions.

The book is structured into eleven gateways, each one focused on a different aspect of prayer. Each gateway has a general introduction followed by numerous recipes. Each recipe appears with inspirational sources and an opening piece that prepare the ground for the actual recipe. At the beginning of each gate, prior to the general introduction, there are prayers from the book *Likutei Tefillot* and selections from contemporary prayer poetry, to open the heart.

The book's initial Gates are dedicated to the different stages of entering prayer and of standing before God. After this there is a look at the different movements of the soul in prayer, and the movements of the body that express prayer. The next Gates relate to the set prayer – the prayer book and communal prayer. The book's last Gates deal with difficulties and obstacles to prayer, and with *hitbodedut*, a person's private prayer from the heart. The concluding Gate is given over to the constant prayer of the soul – at all times and in all places. Although the book's order has an internal logic, it is possible to pick and choose the order of reading it, and to try the different recipes as the heart desires.

Acknowledgments

Blessed is...the One who gave us a true Torah and set in us eternal life.

Obviously, a book is not born from the work of one person alone, and even the individual person is not really alone, but a branch of a whole tree, and thus I wish to express my deep gratitude to many. "Rabbi Ḥanina said: I have learned much from my teachers, from my friends even more, and from my students the most" (Taanit 7a).

My main teachers, Rav Shagar and Rav Menachem Froman, may the memory of the righteous be blessed, and Rav Adin Steinsaltz, may he live long, each one in his own way gave me a renewed acquaintance with "the One who spoke and the world became," and the many ways to serve God and be in real, connected dialogue with Him.

Yeshivat HaKotel and the head of the yeshiva, Rav Hadari of righteous and blessed memory, were my first home of Torah, learning, and prayer.

Thank you to my friends who have been with me for all the long years from Yeshivat HaKotel and Shefa, Makor Chaim, and the *Beit Midrash LeHithadshut* (Study Center for Renewal).

To Yeshivat Makor Chaim, of which I merit to count myself among the founders, and which provided me a warm home and fertile ground for creativity. A special thank you to Rabbi David Rabinowitz, my full partner in leading the yeshiva, and with him the dedicated staff of rabbis and teachers over the many years, and to Avi Sarel, Yossi Baumol, and Eitan Hollander, who are tirelessly devoted to raising the funds and resources necessary for the growing scope of our activities and the construction of our new campus.

To my *havruta* Rabbi Pedaya Nagar, and to Rabbi Yossi Froman, with whom I have walked in recent years in a journey of prayer.

To my students in the yeshiva and in the various *havurot* over the years, who with great patience and limitless presence were with me for endless hours in preparation for prayer, for nights of *hitbodedut*, and journeys to burial places of the righteous. For opening their hearts and agreeing to be the "tasters" of the recipes in their early stages.

To my dear and loving family members, from my elders, my grandfather Zalman Dov Hakohen Berkowitz and his father Rabbi Pinhas, from the town of Satmar and surrounding areas, who were murdered along with the rest of our extended family by the Nazi oppressors, may their memory be obliterated. I was privileged to have them present in my life on a daily basis even though I did not actually merit to meet them.

To my honored parents, Chaim Michael, of blessed memory, and my mother Esther, may she live and be well, who raised me with endless love, trust, and faith.

To my beloved one and only sister, Ziva, to her husband, Eli, and to the entire dear Lamdan family.

To my children, each one of whom is very dear, and all of whom together are my central source of strength. The learning I do with their children is a complete realization of the blessing that a Jew can merit, and for which I thank them greatly.

"And Isaac entreated God in the presence of his wife (Gen. 25:21)" – above all I have merited in the partnership I have with my wife, Iris Zurtel, the best *ḥavruta* I could have in life, in Torah, and in prayer.

To those who were involved in the process of creating this book, among whom I owe particular thanks to two women: The first is Reut Brosh, who wrote, edited, changed, found sources, and essentially transformed what was an oral prayer into a written prayer, and for this I am very grateful to her; I assume that you, who are reading this book, share my gratitude. The second is Leah Hartman, who with exquisite sensitivity to language and deep spiritual understanding endeavored to capture the wind whispering between the words. Every translation is a challenge, but the translation of prayer, whose words hold secrets within them, is exponentially more so, and for this I thank her very much.

To the dear staff of Maggid Books: Matthew and Yehoshua Miller, Rabbi Reuven Ziegler, Shira Finson, Eliyahu Misgav, Nechama Unterman, Rina Ben-Gal and Rachel Kellner, to Stuart Schnee, and all those who took part in the publication of this book, with generosity of spirit and in genuine partnership.

And last but not least, I would like to thank all those who have contributed, both publicly and privately, in myriad ways – giving of their time, money, and wisdom in order to support the activities of Makor Chaim Institutions in general and this book in particular. Thank you very much.

אבוא ביתך

Let Me Enter Your House

Let my prayer rise before You
Like the incense and perfect sacrifices
Offered by those who are whole and perfect.
Master of the world,
Open Your mouth to a mute like me
And allow me to fix my prayer, my supplication,
    and my request before You
As is fitting in every moment
So that I may be able to elucidate what I have to
    say before You always
And everything that is in my heart I shall say
With truth, with pleas, with mercy,
In a way that will awaken Your mercy on me
And You will answer my request with mercy
    always.

Likutei Tefillot, part 1, prayer 14

Then my soul will say with all of my being:
Come greet the bride, dear beloved alight.

If my soul drowns in my tears
Is this not the sign that my destiny nears?

From the day I emerged from my mother's
    womb
I set Your face ever before me,

For I have nothing other than Your hope in the
    world,
For You are my honor, You are my glory,

You like an ember burn on my lips,
And on my pure heart sit like a pearl.

Pinhas Sadeh

פתיחה: נבואה שעריך
Opening: Let Us Enter Your Gates

וַאֲנִי בְּרֹב חַסְדְּךָ אָבוֹא בֵיתֶךָ אֶשְׁתַּחֲוֶה אֶל הֵיכַל קָדְשְׁךָ בְּיִרְאָתֶךָ.

תהלים ה, ח

But I, through Your abundant love, enter Your house; I bow down in awe at Your holy Temple.

Psalms 5:8

[One] should not stand up to pray unless he is in a serious frame of mind. The original pious ones used to wait one hour and then pray, in order to direct their heart toward the Omnipresent.

Mishna Berakhot 5:1

What is meant by [proper] intention? One should clear his mind from all thoughts and envision himself as standing before the Divine Presence. Therefore, one must sit a short while before praying in order to focus his attention and then pray in a pleasant and supplicatory fashion. One should not pray as one carrying a burden who throws it off and walks away. Therefore, one must sit a short while after praying, and then withdraw.

Rambam, *Mishneh Torah, Hilkhot Tefilla UVirkat Kohanim* 4:16

In our prayer we come to the House of God
Stand before the Sovereign
Turn to the One full of mercy,
Give ourselves over to the love of our Beloved.
Prayer is devotion
The devoted pause, preparing the heart before their prayer
Like a musician tuning an instrument before beginning to play,
Hoping for a clear, bright voice.

In the race that is life
In which we run from task to task
Prayer can easily become yet another task.
The secret is in the pause – to arrive early, to sit for a bit.
To move from doing to being,
To quiet the motor
That pushes me constantly
Forward, higher.
To intensify my presence, and that of the world around me,
To calm my mind
To awaken the inner desire concealed deep within
To stand before God
To enter God's gates.

פתיחת החושים
Opening the Senses

For every part of creation has an inner point that was clarified by God's honor.… And this is the meaning of Perek Shira – that each part of creation has its own song and praise for the Blessed God. And "then Israel sang… this song" (Num. 21:17), meaning: the known song that arises from all created things.

Rebbe Yehuda Aryeh Leib Alter of Gur, *Sefat Emet, Beshallaḥ* 5631

All of existence yearns for the source of its life, every plant and every blade of grass, every speck of sand and clump of earth. Everything that reveals life and everything that hides within it life, the small parts of creation and the big, the heavens above and fiery angels, all the details of all being, and the wholeness of it – everything aspires, yearns, longs for the desired wholeness of its supreme, living, holy, pure, powerful source.

Rabbi Avraham Yitzhak HaKohen Kook, *Olat Re'iya, Inyenei Tefilla* 7

The walk to the synagogue
Is the beginning of prayer
It is an invitation to be present
To step inside
To stand before God.
In our day to day we are often a bit fuzzy and imprecise.
The path to prayer is the beginning of the path
To presence, to clarity, to precision.

- Stepping outside, to a field, to a garden, or to any quiet place, we close our eyes, breathe deeply, and listen. We try to gather in the many surrounding sounds, discerning among them: the call of the rooster, the rustle of the wind, the din of cars on the road. Sounds close and far, sounds strong and weak. Smelling the air, the ground, the tree, we allow their scents to enter inside us, and penetrate deeply.

- Opening our eyes, we look about. Trying to notice details that until now have remained hidden, we look out into the expanse, to the sky, to the green trees, to the flowers. We notice the taste in our mouth. We feel the tree, brush the ground, sense the touch of the body.

- We allow the sounds, the smells, the sights, the tastes, and the touch to saturate us, to penetrate deeply, inward.
  We become one with the surrounding existence,
  A part of the universe where prayer is the language, the wellspring,
  The heartbeat of life and its pulse.

- Now our presence is raised immeasurably
  And thus we arrive to the synagogue
  With a wide-open heart.
  A soft step.
  Present.
  Open.

לרוץ לתפילה

Running to Prayer

דֶּרֶךְ־מִצְוֹתֶיךָ אָרוּץ כִּי תַרְחִיב לִבִּי.

תהלים קיט, לב

[In] the way of Your commandments I shall run, for You will broaden my heart.

Psalms 119:32

It is a mitzva to run when going to the synagogue, just as it is a mitzva to hurry to do any mitzvot, but it should be done in a way that does not arouse ridicule from those who see. Rather one should go as one goes quickly to their work. And our rabbis of blessed memory said about the verse "A king is bound in the tresses" that the Divine Presence is tied to the Jewish people in their exile because of two times that Abraham, our holy father, ran for a mitzva. For it is written: "And Abraham went quickly to the tent, to Sarah," "And Abraham ran to the cattle." And it is also said in the holy Zohar that when Israel runs to do a mitzva, the angels of defense run opposite them, and go early to tell of their merit. However, one should only run until the entrance of the synagogue, but in the synagogue itself it is forbidden to run. Rather one should walk with awe and fear, for it is the shrine of the King of Glory.

Rabbi Yosef Hayim of Baghdad, *Ben Ish Ḥai, Hilkhot Shana Rishona, Parashat Miketz*, 2

Morning
The sun rises
The alarm rings

It's hard to get up
Arousing ourselves
We open our eyes
We give thanks
What awaits us today?
All of the day's pressure and burdens rest upon our shoulders
Sometimes, on a day of grace
We can suddenly feel our soul yearning for its Creator

We want to breathe deeply
To make the day last
The feet, without prompting, begin to run
Quickly
To the House of Prayer
To stand before the Master of All
To do God's will
To run.

- Choose one day of the week, wake up early and get ready quickly. Head to the synagogue, as quickly as possible, if you can – running.
- Upon arrival, stop, steady your breath, fill yourself with awe of the space.
- Recite the verse: "And I, through Your abundant kindness, will enter Your house; I will prostrate myself toward Your Holy Sanctuary in awe of You" (Ps. 5:8). Enter inside, begin to pray.

יהי רצון

May It Be Your Desire

יִהְיוּ לְרָצוֹן אִמְרֵי פִי.

תהלים יט, טו

May the sayings of my mouth be desirable.

Psalms 19:15

But, as for me, may my prayer to You, O Lord, be in a time of desire. O God, with Your abundant kindness, answer me with the truth of Your salvation.

Psalms 69:14

The main aspect of prayer is the revelation of desire, the aspect of "But as for me, may my prayer to You, O Lord, be in a time of desire."

Rebbe Natan of Breslov, *Likutei Halakhot, Hilkhot Birkhot HaShaḥar* 5

So what do you want today?
A person is defined not only by action
But first and foremost by desire.
It's as if prayer is telling me: Be impractical.
Every one of us walks about the world with desires hidden
 deep within,
Desires awaiting prayer.
Prayer is an opportunity
To sojourn in the realm of desires
Without forcing them
Without seeking the means to pull them down into the world
 of action
Simply to be in the world of expressing desires.

We tell the Holy Blessed One our dreams
About what we want today:
I want to be happy
I want to speak truth
I want to see Jerusalem rebuilt.

Just as in the Torah there are many layers – the simple
 meaning, the deeper explanations, the hints, the secrets
And one can choose which layer to understand,
 to be in right now,
So in life there are dimensions of existence
And one of these is the world of desires.
Prayer gives me the chance to linger in this world.
 To make space for desire.

To let my desire sprout on the fertile soil of prayer
To water it
To let it grow
Slowly.

- Imagine the desires that move through your mind like waves in the sea.

- Write down the desires that arise, all of them, as they are.

- Among all the desires that arise, "catch" one, like catching a wave. With this one desire, begin working: identify it, rouse it, try to understand it fully.

- Write down whatever else comes up in the moment in relation to this desire, and describe it.

- After the desire has sprouted and become clear, allow a prayer to grow out of it. A prayer that remains in the realm of revealed desire and expressed in words, without worrying how it will come to fruition in reality.

מציאת חן

Finding Favor

וְנֹחַ מָצָא חֵן בְּעֵינֵי ה': כֵּן נִמְצָא חֵן וְשֵׂכֶל טוֹב בְּעֵינֵי אֱלֹהִים וְאָדָם.

בראשית ו, ח, הבדלה בנוסח עדות המזרח

And Noah found favor in the eyes of the Lord: May we find favor and good mind in the eyes of God and humans.

Genesis 6:8, Sephardic text of Havdala

For indeed this is the work of man – to find favor in the eyes of God, and then God helps those who walk wholeheartedly.

Rebbe Yehuda Aryeh Leib Alter of Gur, *Sefat Emet, Noaḥ* 5647

For the main reason requests are not accepted is that our words lack grace and do not penetrate the heart of the one being asked. It is as if there's no place in his heart for the words to enter.

Rebbe Nahman of Breslov, *Likutei Moharan*, part 1, torah 1

Speech between two people is a two-way street
I speak, say what is in my heart
Checking all the time: Are my words being heard? Have they been received? Are they being understood?
Words that find favor are words that speak to the heart.
We don't always remember this, but when we stand before God,
Our prayer needs not only to be said, but to be received. To find favor.

In order for the words of our prayer to be received,
It is not enough to just say them, to read them straight from the prayer book.
We must find favor
To open space in the heart of the listener,
To awaken a desire to hear our prayer.
To a child who asks us for something, we instruct: "Say please," "Say thank you."
There is a way to say what is in our heart, a way to request, a way to thank, a way to express wonder.
When we consider how we are using our words to find favor, we will begin to listen to the melody of the words,
To the wording of the prayer, to the expressions of the mouth.

- Choose a specific section of the daily prayer to focus on today.
- Read it slowly.
- Now give consideration to the melody of the words, the emphasis we place on them, how to pray the words in such a way that others will want to hear them.
- Choose on which words to pause, which ones to say quickly. Choose the proper tune for today.
- Attempt to add grace to the words,
- To find favor.
- Try again and again, until you have been successful.

לפני ולפנים

All the Way In

אֵין זֶה כִּי אִם בֵּית אֱלֹהִים וְזֶה שַׁעַר הַשָּׁמָיִם.

בראשית כח, יז

This is none other than the house of God, and this is the gate of heaven.

Genesis 28:17

A person should always enter a distance of two doorways into the synagogue and then pray.

Berakhot 8a

Fortunate is the man who listens to me to watch by my doors day by day, to watch the doorposts of my entrances.

Proverbs 8:34

What does it mean "to watch by my doors"? The Holy Blessed One said, "If you went to pray in the synagogue, do not stand at the outer entrance to pray, rather intend to go inside, door after door." It does not say "to watch by my door" but "my doors" – two doors.

Deuteronomy Rabba, *Ki Tavo, parasha* 7

The entrance into prayer
Doesn't happen in a single moment.
It needs us to step into it
From the outside in, all the way in.
Entering the holy space is a kind of going inside, step by step,
Gateway upon gateway.
Hence our great teachers built the prayer book
Layer by layer:
There are the initial stages of the prayer that bring me inside,
Preparing, inviting,
And there are pinnacle moments of meeting
That take place only once I am already inside, immersed,
    deeply.
After the peak there is a gradual leave-taking.
Inside our soul there exists a similar pattern of entering,
    of being ready.
This existing pattern within us connects to the way our prayer
    is designed.
Being aware of this inner soul movement of "entering in" can
    aid us in our entrance,
Sensing prayer as dynamic rather than linear,
As a living event, full of movement.

In order to deepen our awareness of the entrance into prayer and its different stages, let's explore different kinds of entrances we experience:

- Choose an "entrance into": entering into your home, bringing in Shabbat, stepping into a wedding, etc.

- Try to identify four stages of entering, from the outside in.

  For example, the four stages of entering into a home:

  Stage 1 – Parking the car outside.

  Stage 2 – Standing at front door, wiping your shoes.

  Stage 3 – Opening the door, kissing the mezuza.

  Stage 4 – Greeting all those present with a blessing, with a hug.

  Pay attention to the moment you begin to gradually end the process of entering into your home, and go on to a different stage – being at home.

- Once you've gained experience noticing these stages in different kinds of "enterings" of day-to-day life, contemplate one of the daily prayers, attempting to notice the entrance into it:

  At one point does the prayer begin for you?

  What makes up the prayer?

  What challenges you in entering into the prayer?

  What helps you to enter in?

דע לפני מי אתה עומד

Know Before Whom You Stand

May I believe with perfect faith
That the world is filled with Your glory
And that when we pray, You stand before us
And You hear and listen and notice
 Every word of our prayer.
May I know before whom I stand
Before the King of kings, the Holy Blessed
 One.
As a result, may I experience fear and awe
 before You,
May I have profound intent in my every word
 of prayer,
May I not lose my focus at all on any word of
 the prayer.

Likutei Tefillot, part 1, prayer 84

In the Beginning
Rivka Miriam

In the Beginning God created
The Heavens that essentially are not
And the earth that wants to touch them,
In the Beginning God created
Strings stretched
Between them
Between the Heavens that essentially are not
And the land that longs,
And man God created
For the man is prayer and a thread touching
That which is not
With a soft and subtle touch.

פתיחה: לעמוד לנוכח
Opening: Standing Present

אֲנִי בְּצֶדֶק אֶחֱזֶה פָנֶיךָ אֶשְׂבְּעָה בְהָקִיץ תְּמוּנָתֶךָ.

תהלים יז, טו

I will see Your face with righteousness; I will be satisfied with Your image upon the awakening.

Psalms 17:15

One who prays must direct his eyes downward and his heart upward.

Yevamot 105b

Standing before God
With words
With silence
In fear and trembling
Awe and love
Sharpening our gaze
Opening our hands
Standing upright on two feet
Heightening our presence
Feeling God's presence with us
Calling out God's name
Wanting to come together, to come close
To know our Maker
To know
Before Whom
We stand.

הכרת הנוכח
Perceiving the Presence

שִׁפְכִי כַמַּיִם לִבֵּךְ נֹכַח פְּנֵי ה'.

איכה ב, יט

Pour out your heart like water before the presence of the Lord.

Lamentations 2:19

If you prepare your heart and spread out your hands to Him.

Job 11:13

What is intention?
That one should empty his heart of all thoughts and see himself as if he is standing before the Shekhina.
Therefore one should sit a bit before prayer in order to direct his heart.

Rambam, *Hilkhot Tefilla* 4:16

Prayer
Even before it is a request,
Even before it is an expression of gratitude,
Even before it is praise,
Is an encounter.
Standing in the presence,
Before the *Shekhina*, God's indwelling presence.
Therefore, the first step we take as we enter into prayer
Is the opening of consciousness to presence,
To the sense that God is here
Above me, in front of me, around me, inside of me.
To the knowledge that all things I see around me are not only inanimate objects,
Rather they hold within them deep desire and yearning.
To the sense that each and every person surrounding me truly exists,
Present and full of longing.
And the Source of Life is also here,
Reachable, close, touching.

The awareness of another's presence can be felt on the simplest level by working in pairs:

- Define roles at the outset – one is present, the other gives presence.

- Sit together for a few minutes.
  The present one is present,
  Focusing on the very essence of their existence.
  Breathing deeply and slowly, relaxing the body, letting go of all thoughts.
  The one who gives presence is aware,
  Trying to feel the very presence of the other,
  Not their thoughts, not their desires,
  Not who they are, or what they are.
  Rather to sense their actual presence,
  To let this presence impact, pass through, envelop.

- When ready,
  The one giving presence should turn to the present one and say: Y O U.
  Once, twice, three times, ten times.

- The addressing of the other as "you"
  Is not what creates their presence,
  But is rather an acknowledgment of the realness of it,
  An awakening to their very existence.
  Even prior to the addressing of the other,
  It connects the present one and the one who gives presence.

- The present one allows the calling out of Y O U to permeate their being, to penetrate their heart, until they open their mouth and answer I.

- At a more advanced stage, alone or with a partner, we progress to sensing the Divine Presence surrounding us, peering at us from every object, from every tree, from every breeze.
  We allow it to encircle us, to embrace us, to wrap itself around our being.

- In this way we will build within us the primary Y O U, the most basic, the one we will use each time we say "Blessed are Y O U" in our prayer.
  The existing, the present Y O U, that fills all worlds.

- It is important to realize that we can't force this feeling of presence, and we can't know when it will come.
  Yet the intention opens the gates of our heart to it, and enables its existence.

אני, אתה והוא

I, You, and He

כִּי אָנוּ עַמֶּךָ וְאַתָּה אֱלֹהֵינוּ...

For we are Your people and You are our God
We are Your children and You are our Father
We are Your servants and You are our Master
We are Your gathering and You are our Place
We are Your legacy and You are our Land
We are Your flock and You are our Shepherd
We are Your vineyard and You are our Keeper
We are Your work and You are our Maker
We are Your bride and You are our Lover
We are Your treasure and You are our God
We are Your people and You are our King
We give You our word and You give us Yours
Our days are like a fleeting shadow
But You are here and Your years will not end.

From the Yom Kippur prayers

Blessed are You, God.
This is I, the one speaking to You,
Toward You.
The conversation between us is different each day,
Each moment,
Because I am constantly changing,
And You also reveal Yourself to me with Your infinite faces.
As I stand to pray
I wonder who am I
Turning to You, seeking Your face, feeling out who are Y O U.

- We can begin with "I":
  Closing your eyes, sit quietly for a few moments.
  Breathe slowly,
  Try to sense yourself now,
  What you are feeling,
  What expresses you in this moment.
  From here will come the direct, exact address for your prayer.
  I...and You?
  For example: I am sad, and You are the essence of joy.
  Or perhaps: I am sad, and You hold my sadness.
  Or maybe even: I am sad, and You are indifferent.

- At times I am not so connected to myself, and my own sense of "I" is dim.
  So here it's good to try the opposite, and begin by sensing the "You," and from the "You" the "I" will become clear.
  You...and I?
  For example: You are truth, and I am full of lies.
  Or perhaps: You are truth, and I am making an effort, I am trying.
  Or maybe even: You are the essential truth, and I am a little bit of truth.

- Once You and I are both present, we can take one step further, for God is not only standing in front of me, present before me, part of our conversation, but rather God is infinite, bigger than this present moment, looking out over the "I-You."

God is the Present Hidden One. Filling all worlds and surrounding all worlds, concealed and hidden.

When we want to bring in the perspective of the *ein sof*, the infinite and beyond, into our prayer, Hebrew uses the masculine pronoun to do so, and calls God *Hu*, meaning "He." This pronoun denotes something beyond us, something we can't address with the more intimate "You."

- Once we have clarified the "I" and the "You," we can add in the "He" according to how we experience it in the moment.

  I…You…and He?

  For example: I am sad, You comfort me, and He remains quiet.

  Or perhaps: I aim for truth, You are the essential truth, and He is beyond everything.

  Or maybe even: I am trying, You are occupied with Your business, and He contemplates everything, and knows the secret.

קריאה בשם

Calling by Name

קָרוֹב ה׳ לְכָל קֹרְאָיו לְכֹל אֲשֶׁר יִקְרָאֻהוּ בֶאֱמֶת.

תהלים קמה, יח

The Lord is near to all who call Him, to all who call Him with sincerity.

Psalms 145:18

*I shall fortify him because he knows My name.
He will call Me and I shall answer him.*

Psalms 91:14–15

Why do the people of Israel pray but are not answered? Rabbi Yehoshua ben Levi said in the name of Rabbi Pinḥas ben Yair: For they do not know the secret of the explicit name.

Pesikta Rabbati, piska 22:7

In our prayer we call out to God
Asking God to be attentive to us.
We don't want to speak to the void, to just move our lips.
We turn to God and ask:
Hear God, my voice when I call.
Be with me. Hear me. Listen closely to me.

Being called, like being loved, creates a sense of great arousal.
When I call out to you, or I call out to You,
This calling by name weaves an invisible string between us,

Reminding us of the link and the connection between us.
Our prayer book is full of God's names:
Great One, Master of the World, My Soul's Beloved, Healer of the Sick, Sovereign of all Sovereigns, Hearer of Prayer, Builder of Jerusalem, Hashem, Our Lord in Heaven, *Tatte*.
So many names.
An infinite number of names. An infinite number of faces.
Each name opens me up to a different revelation of God.
Each name holds within it a different secret.
Each name reveals another little bit of my connection with God.
The calling out of God's name in prayer is like a tug on a hidden rope
Stretched from the Heavens to the Earth
And just saying the name already invites a meeting between us, awakening us to connection.

- When we rise for our personal prayer, we scan the pages for the most exact name, looking for the name that is most fitting in this moment.

- Everyone should ask themselves:
  To Whom am I turning,
  Before Whom am I standing,
  To Whom am I speaking,
  Whom am I inviting,
  To Whom am I calling out?

- From within the plethora of God's names, choose as exactly as possible the one that fits your prayer in this moment.

תפילה כעמידה למשפט
Prayer as Standing in Judgment

כְּבַקָּרַת רוֹעֶה עֶדְרוֹ מַעֲבִיר צֹאנוֹ תַּחַת שִׁבְטוֹ...

As a shepherd herds his flock, directing his sheep to pass under his staff, so do You pass, count, and record the souls of every living thing.

From the prayer *UNetaneh Tokef* – Rosh HaShana prayers

My son, when you enter before your Creator, enter with fear and awe. And when you pray, know before Whom you stand.

Otzar HaMidrashim, page 29

"I have set the Lord before me constantly" (Ps. 16:8); this is a major principle in the Torah and amongst the virtues of the righteous who walk before God. For a person's way of sitting, his movements, and his dealings while he is alone in his house are not like his way of sitting, his movements, and his dealings when he is before a great king; nor are his speech and free expression as much as he wants when he is with the household members and his relatives like his speech when in a royal audience. All the more so when one takes to heart that the Great King, the Holy One, blessed is He, Whose glory fills the earth, is standing over him and watching his actions, as it is stated, "'Will a man hide in concealment and I will not see him?' – the word of God" (Jer. 23:24), he immediately acquires awe and submission in fear of God, May He be Blessed, and feels shame before Him constantly.

Rabbi Moshe Isserles (Rema), *Shulḥan Arukh, Oraḥ Ḥayim, Hilkhot Hanhagat Adam BaBoker*, 1

Standing before God
Who searches the kidneys and the heart, the emotions and the thoughts,
Standing as the accused
Before the One Judge of the World,
Standing
Appealing.

Coming to be seen before God
To be seen
To be counted
To be remembered.

Standing subdued
Transparent
Allowing the Divine gaze to penetrate me
Without responding, without explaining, without offering excuses,
Justifying the judgment.

- Stand upright, like the accused before a judge.
- Close your eyes and allow yourself to be filled with the sense that we are all completely transparent, and with an inquiring gaze our mysteries can be perceived. We stand, and invite the Divine gaze to rest on us, to assess us.
  Quieting the voices buzzing within, we give ourselves over to this Divine gaze, allowing it to envelop us, to probe us, and to judge us.
- After opening our eyes, we can write down the "decree": What did I sense when the Divine gaze saw me today?

Silence

שתיקה

לְךָ דֻמִיָּה תְהִלָּה.

תהלים סה, ב

Silence is praise to You.

Psalms 65:2

In prayer, we are accustomed to uttering words,
To filling the void.
But even when standing before God
We are allowed to be quiet
To do nothing.
To cease trying
To not fear the quiet
To give space to the embarrassment
To the awe
To stand silently
Still
Awakening my attention
To my very existence.
A person
Between ground and sky
Placing God before me
A taut string between us
In silence.

- Stand before God in a prayer that is all silence. (Begin with only two minutes, but, in time, you can lengthen this.)
  A restful silence, like the kind shared with a good friend with whom you can just sit without saying anything, an island of quiet amongst a sea of words.

- Hold everything that arises, everything that happens.

- At the end of the set time, write down all that came up in the quiet.

תנועות הנפש בתפילה

Soul Movements in Prayer

My King and my God
I will pray to You
I will cry out to You
I will plead with You
I will prostrate myself before You.
Before You "I will prostrate myself and bow
 down. I will bend my knee before God Who
 made me."
I stretched my hands out to You, "I spread out
 my hands all day long, my soul turns to You
 like a weary land."
My heart will cry out to God.
From the depths of my heart I call to You,
From the deepest depths I beg for Your true
 compassion and graciousness.
"Like a deer yearning along the channels of
 water,
so does my soul yearn for You, God."
Like doves moaning, "beating their breasts,"
So does my heart moan for Your vast compassion and kindness.
"As a lion or young lion growls over his prey,
though a band of shepherds gathers against him,

he does not fear their voice and is not
    subdued by their stirring."
So shall I roar, cry out, moan, yearn,
    call, hope, and wait
For Your compassion and salvation.
I will not be silent
I will always call out to You.

Likutei Tefillot, part 2, prayer 5

Longing
Miriam Barukh Halfi

And there was a longing in me
And it had no boundary

It didn't have
A boundary to be stopped
It didn't have
A boundary of calm

And I made in myself
boundaries, boundaries
At which to stop and to see.

And I carved in me
Stairs upon stairs
To see the sky

And a ray of calm touched me.

פתיחה: ניגון הלב
Opening: Song of the Heart

וְעַתָּה קְחוּ לִי מְנַגֵּן וְהָיָה כְּנַגֵּן הַמְנַגֵּן וַתְּהִי עָלָיו יַד ה'.

מלכים ב ג, טו

"And now bring me a musician." And it was that when the musician played, the hand of the Lord came upon him.

II Kings 3:15

The word *ruaḥ* means spirit, and also breath.
When we pray, we are tuning our inner spirit,
We are directing the breath of God that blows within us.
A master of prayer is like a musician
Who when playing
Transforms the whispers of the inner cavern
Into a song of the yearnings of the soul, of the longings of the
    heart,
Into prayer.

Before beginning to play
We must tune our instrument
Find the right pitch
Check our spirits
What's flowing through us.

I can pray in the spirit with which I woke this morning,
Or I can allow the prayer to inspire me,
To teach me how a person should feel in this world,
To allow the spirit to move through me, drawing the notes out
    of me.

Each stage of our prayer attunes us to a different flow of spirit,
    to another melody.
The flute's music shifts:
From the joy of gratitude, to the song of praise,
From the murmur of pleading, to the cry, or the silence.
We are listening to the spirit,
Tuning our instrument to the song of the heart.

Giving Thanks

תודה

מוֹדִים אֲנַחְנוּ לָךְ...

We give thanks to You,
For You
Are the Lord our God and God of our ancestors
For ever and all time,
You are the Rock of our lives
Shield of our salvation
From generation to generation.
We will thank You and declare Your praise
For our lives which are entrusted into Your hand
For our souls which are placed in Your charge
For Your miracles which are with us every day
And for Your wonders and favors at all times, evening,
morning, and midday.

From the prayer *Modim*

We give thanks to You our God...
For that we may thank You.

From the prayer *Modim DeRabbanan*

In the future
All the Temple offerings will be nullified
With one exception – the thanksgiving offering.
When no words are left
Only one thing will remain:
Giving thanks.

We think that one who receives says thank you,
But really the opposite is true:
The one who says thank you is the true recipient.
This person knows how to receive.

When I say thank you,
I first of all receive.
I accept my reality,
All that is happening to me.
I know that I am all that I am,
And I deserve nothing more.
I accept the love, the plenty,
Happy with what is.
Everything that was up 'til now, everything that is right now –
Nothing is to be taken for granted.
And when, nevertheless, something is given to me, anything –
I accept,
I expand,
I am filled,
I give thanks
Not only for what I've received, but also for the simple ability to give thanks.

- Taking a piece of paper and a pen, we write out a list,
  Ten points of gratitude, maybe more, maybe less,
  Things we've been given and are happy with, grateful for, no matter how big or how small.

- We read them out loud, one by one, and give thanks for them from the bottom of our heart.

- After the initial reading, we go back and repeat our thanks from the beginning.
  We say them again, this time expanding on them, detailing each one of the items.
  We open our hearts, allowing the gratitude to be present within us,
  To echo inside of us
  From the head to the heart, from the heart to the entire body,
  Strong,
  Filling.

- And when all of the bones will give thanks,
  We can add to our words a slight gesture,
  Perhaps a bow, perhaps spreading open our hands.
  Thank You.

שבח

Praise

וְאִלּוּ פִינוּ מָלֵא שִׁירָה כַּיָּם...

If our mouths were as full of song as the sea,
And our tongue with jubilation as is myriad waves,
If our lips were full of praise like the spacious heavens,
And our eyes shone like the sun and moon,
If our hands were outstretched like eagles of the sky,
And our feet as swift as hinds –
Still we could not thank You enough,
Lord our God and God of our ancestors,
Or bless Your name
  For even one of the thousand thousands and myriad myriads of favors
You did for our ancestors and for us.

From the prayer *Nishmat Kol Ḥai*

I look around me.
The world is full of stars and the solar system
And the wonders of nature
And technology
And incredible people.
Wow.
It is incredible what is happening here.
What a wondrous world.

Praise is the movement of amazement,
Of awe.
Opening the eyes to the wonder of creation.
I pray
And I sing
I extol
And I say
And my mouth is full of song.

I am flooded
My emotions overflow.
Wow.
You are worthy of praise.

In order to fill ourselves with the feeling of praise, we will use the structure of the traditional prayer *Barukh SheAmar* – "Blessed is the One who spoke."

- Beginning with the first line of the prayer, say:
  Blessed is the One who spoke and the world came to be, Blessed is the One.
  And we add to this, additional expressions of praise:
  Blessed is the One who…
  Blessed is the One who…
  Blessed is the One who…
  For example:
  Blessed is the One who created the wondrous human body.
  Blessed is the One who created such a beautiful world.
  Blessed is the One who fashioned the human mind.
  Blessed is the One who brought the power of healing into the world.

One can experiment with this template in a group as well:

- Heading outdoors together, we dedicate several minutes to becoming filled with feelings of praise and wonder. Looking at our lives, at our surroundings, we are awed.

- After some time, we come together in a circle.

- We say together: Blessed is the One who spoke and the world came to be, Blessed is the One. Next, each person in turn opens with these words: "Blessed is the One who…" and says a word of praise to the Holy Blessed One. Instead of "Amen" everyone answers, "Wow," or any other expression of amazement. Continue thus, one after the other.

תחנונים

Supplications

תַּחֲנוּנִים יְדַבֶּר רָשׁ.

משלי יח, כג

A poor man speaks with supplications.

Proverbs 18:23

I plead before You with a voice of screaming, of sighing, of tears.
With every kind of supplication I throw my prayer to You,
My God and God of my fathers, Please! I beg of You before Your Throne of Glory!
With all kinds of voices I call out to You,
I cry to you. Have pity! Have mercy! Be kind to me! Save me!

Rebbe Natan of Breslov, *Likutei Tefillot* 1:23

Our ability to plead is connected to our ability to be in a space that is vulnerable,

Weak,

Needy,

Humble.

To open in our hearts the longing that beats within us,

To allow the tears to be a part of our lives,

So they shouldn't become closed inside of us and become sadness or anger.

To pour our heart out before God

Like a child pleading to a parent.

To request again
To beg
To awaken grace
To request an undeserved gift:
I want to continue to live
I want to live better
I want to draw down health to those in need
I want peace.
I'm pleading.

To linger in the place of the entreaty,
Not to let go,
To say unequivocally: This is precious to me, I am asking, I am begging.
To allow myself to cry
The tears are precious
Tears have the power to open all of the gates,
To awaken mercy.

- Choosing something that you really, really want, state it as a request.

- Say it several times, each time changing the intensity of the request and the entreaty. Say it strongly, say it gently. Pray more and more intensely, as if you are turning an inner dial that controls the potency of the prayer, alternately raising and lowering the volume.

- The last stage is to say the plea without the content of the request, but rather with words of entreaty alone (for example: Please, Please, Please).

כיסופים
Yearnings

צָמְאָה לְךָ, נַפְשִׁי, כָּמַהּ לְךָ בְשָׂרִי...

O God, You are my God, I seek You,
My soul thirsts for You, my flesh longs for You.
In an arid and thirsty land, without water.

Psalms 63:2

And know! It is not enough for a person to just long in the heart. He has to express his yearnings orally. To this end, the prayers were established.

Rebbe Nahman of Breslov, *Likutei Moharan*, part 1, torah 31

There is a mountain. On the mountain there is a stone. From this stone flows a Spring. Everything has a Heart. Therefore, the world as a whole also has a Heart.

The mountain with the stone and the Spring stands at one end of the world. The Heart of the World stands at the opposite end of the world. The Heart of the World faces the Spring and constantly longs and yearns to come to the Spring. It has a very, very great longing, and it cries out very much that it should be able to come to the Spring and the Spring also yearns for the Heart.

Rebbe Nahman of Breslov, *Sipurei Maasiyot*, from "The Story of the Seven Beggars"

Sometimes one prays and prays, and this prayer gives voice to
>   their yearnings.
It is the instrument of the call of the heart, to the expanse
That is beyond all distance
Like a bird on a wire
Chirping, wishing
For the bird in a far-off land
And it's as if the call connects them.
Like the heart longing for the spring, for the source of its life
And the yearning is the secret of its strength.

Like a bride and groom on the eve of their wedding
Their words weaving between them a delicate pining,
>   entwined with words of yearning.

In the place where the distance is infinite
Words of prayer create closeness
And longing turns to devotion.

- Pausing for several minutes, we listen to the yearnings that beat within.

- Choose one thing that arises, something that in the moment doesn't seem attainable, but you very much want it and ask for it often (like finding a spouse, or having a child, the building of the Holy Temple, or peace in the Holy Land).

- Looking at this desire from afar, we imagine ourselves in one place, and our desire in another, far-away place with a taut string drawn between us. We feel how the distance between us and the object of our desire, despite the pain that is there, is a kind of connection that bridges between us and the Holy Blessed One.

- Write down the words of your yearnings and your expectations, and pray about what you've written. A prayer that remains in the place of desire, without requesting, for now, the solution or the fix, but rather expressing a readiness to be, for the moment, in a place of yearning.

Crying Out
צעקה

שַׁוְעָתֵנוּ קַבֵּל וּשְׁמַע צַעֲקָתֵנוּ יוֹדֵעַ תַּעֲלוּמוֹת.

מתוך הפיוט "אנא בכוח"

Accept our plea and heed our cry, You Who knows all secret thoughts.

From the *piyut Ana BeKhoaḥ*

Crying out is greater than them all, for crying out is in the heart, as it is written (Lam. 2:18): "Their heart cried out to God"... and this is closer to God than prayer and sighing, for it is written (Ex. 22:22): "For if he cries out to Me, I will surely hear his cry."

Zohar, section 2, 19:2

In prayer we speak,
Transform thoughts and feelings, intentions and movements
    of the soul
Into letters, words, and sentences.
But at times, this is not accessible to us,
Not relevant,
Perhaps because the pain is too deep,
Or perhaps we've forgotten how to speak,
And we don't know how to express ourselves through it.
We are here, God is here,
Only the communication has been cut, lost.
In the place where there are no words – there is a cry,
The cry that existed even before there was speech.
And not infrequently – even when it is possible to speak – it is
    better to cry out.
Crying out is the foundation of communication.
It precedes language.
Even a person who can't speak can cry out.
Even a person whose speech is impaired is able to yell.
How great is crying out,
For it reveals the mysteries of the heart,
It comes before God,
It is heard before God,
It is received.

One possibility:

- Sitting with a partner,
  Each one thinks to themselves:
  What do I have to cry out about?
  What is hidden so deep inside of me that only a cry can get it out of me?

- We tell one another, and talk about it:
  What is stopping me from crying out?
  What could help release it?

- Afterward,

- You imagine yourself crying out.

- An inner scream, a cry from the heart.

- One who is having trouble doing so could cry out for the ability to cry…

Another possibility:

- Head out to the woods, or to the garden, or sit in a car, alone.
  Or go out to a different place that allows you to release the inner scream.
  Alone.

- Open by talking freely to God,
  Sharing what you'd like to cry out about.
  Say it again, with more determination.
  Say it again, this time more softly, pleading.

- Now we scream. Embedding in our voice everything that is going on inside of us, allowing it to come out, without any inhibitions, without any words, loudly, with a raw cry.

- We wait.

- We scream again, this time from the heart alone, from an inner place, soundless.
  We wait, listening inward:
  What was cleansed? What was released?
  Another possibility, for those with the ability to listen deeply, is to wait for an echo, to listen for a response.

תפילות אבות
The Prayers of Our Forefathers

בָּרוּךְ אַתָּה ה׳, אֱלֹהֵינוּ וֵאלֹהֵי אֲבוֹתֵינוּ, אֱלֹהֵי אַבְרָהָם, אֱלֹהֵי יִצְחָק וֵאלֹהֵי יַעֲקֹב.

תפילת עמידה, ברכת אבות

Blessed are You, our God and God of our fathers, God of Abraham, God of Isaac, and God of Jacob.

Amida prayer, *Birkat Avot*

Rabbi Yosei ben Rabbi Ḥanina said: Prayers were instituted by the Patriarchs.... Abraham instituted the morning prayer, as it is stated (Gen. 19:27): "And Abraham rose early in the morning to the place where he had stood," and standing means nothing other than prayer, as it is stated (Ps. 106:30): "And Pinhas stood up and prayed"; Isaac instituted the afternoon prayer, as it is stated (Gen. 24:63): "And Isaac went out to converse [lasuaḥ] in the field toward evening," and conversation means nothing other than prayer, as it is stated (Ps. 102:1): "A prayer of the afflicted when he is faint and pours out his complaint [siḥo] before the Lord"; Jacob instituted the evening prayer, as it is stated (Gen. 28:11): "And he encountered [vayifga] the place and he slept there," and encounter means nothing other than prayer, as it is stated (Jer. 7:16): "And you, do not pray on behalf of this nation and do not raise on their behalf song and prayer, and do not encounter [tifga] Me."

Berakhot 26b

Three forefathers
Bequeathed us
Three prayers.
Each prayer shone in a different light of the day
In sunlight, twilight, or moonlight.
Each prayer was born of a different movement of the soul
As a standing, a conversation, or an encounter.
Each prayer merged from the mountain, from the field,
    or from the home.
Three fathers
Expanded for us the concept of prayer,
Paved paths for us to follow,
Paths to prayer.

עומד על שלו: אברהם

Standing for Himself: Abraham

וַיַּשְׁכֵּם אַבְרָהָם בַּבֹּקֶר אֶל הַמָּקוֹם אֲשֶׁר עָמַד שָׁם אֶת פְּנֵי ה'.

בראשית יט, כז

And Abraham arose early in the morning to the place where he had stood before the Lord.

Genesis 19:27

Abraham rises in the morning
At the day's dawn,
With its clearness,
And stands.
He stands up for himself, he has what to say.
He does not back down, does not give up, does not only prostrate before God and exalt.
He wants to be a partner.
The Hebrew word *pilel* is connected to the word *lehitpallel*, to pray, and also means to appeal in court.

So Abraham appeals – there is a trial taking place.
He has a case and a judgment.
He does not give in, he demands.
Trying to rescue,
He argues.
With courage,
Resolve,
He stands.

Walking in the steps of Abraham, we grasp onto the hem of his robe:

- Beginning in a sitting position, we say a word of thanks or praise to God.
  Now we rise to our feet,
  Feeling our body straightening to full stature.

- We open with Abraham's words, standing before God: "Behold now I have commenced to speak to the Lord, although I am dust and ashes"
  (Gen. 18:27).

- We choose a topic we feel we are already in the process of discussing with God, and for a short while, we beg for it. An issue that we want to stand on, that we are willing to argue about, to demand of God.
  We spell out our demand in detail, repeating it a number of times, firmly and humbly.

- When we finish, we take three steps back, express our gratitude and sit down.

שיחה: יצחק
Conversation: Isaac

וַיֵּצֵא יִצְחָק לָשׂוּחַ בַּשָּׂדֶה לִפְנוֹת עָרֶב וַיִּשָּׂא עֵינָיו וַיַּרְא וְהִנֵּה גְמַלִּים בָּאִים.

בראשית כד, סג

And Isaac went forth to pray in the field toward evening, and he lifted his eyes and saw, and behold, camels were approaching.

Genesis 24:63

Isaac goes out to converse in the field.
In a prayer that holds within it the gentleness of the field, the connection to the natural flow, the continuing conversation of nature and the world.
As evening falls, as the sun sets
Nature is at its most beautiful
Painted in colors of yearning.
Isaac is in deep conversation, speaking heart to heart.
He pours out his speech before the Lord
Without effort, without force, without judgment.
This simple sharing becomes the raw material of the connection with God.
The commonplace and the mundane are transformed into the infinite.

And there is One who hears and answers. There is an echo.
   A conversation.
In just a moment Isaac will meet Rebecca.
This conversation in the field is also the opening of the heart to relationship,
To the words and conversation that form it.
Isaac and Rebecca are like two leaves blowing in the wind,
Like two birds on a wire,
Conversing.

- Stepping outside to an open space, we notice the nature surrounding us, the blowing of the wind whispering in the trees,
  We listen to the chirping of the birds.

- Now we bring our personal voice into the great discussion taking place, we become a part of the music.
  We allow our words to flow forth from us, pouring out our soul.
  We share with God what arises for us in this moment
  Without asking for anything,
  Without trying,
  Simply talking
  With an open heart.

אל מול הקיר: יעקב

Up Against the Wall: Jacob

וַיִּפְגַּע בַּמָּקוֹם וַיָּלֶן שָׁם כִּי בָא הַשֶּׁמֶשׁ וַיִּקַּח מֵאַבְנֵי הַמָּקוֹם וַיָּשֶׂם מְרַאֲשֹׁתָיו וַיִּשְׁכַּב בַּמָּקוֹם הַהוּא.

בראשית כח, יא

And he arrived at the place and lodged there because the sun had set, and he took some of the stones of the place and placed [them] at his head, and he lay down in that place.

Genesis 28:11

The whole world became like a wall before him.

Genesis Rabba 68:10

Jacob flees
Alone
At night
In a time of despair, of doubt,
He doesn't see how to go forward.
He collides with the place,
Stuck.
Being stuck, this impasse
Transforms into prayer.
Yaakov is stuck in place, and discovers that this is *the* place,
The place that is the Place of the World.

This wall he's hit becomes the Wailing Wall,
The collision becomes connection.
When we hit a wall and cannot move forward
We have no choice but to turn our eyes upward
And suddenly our field of vision expands
Everything becomes possible.
The limit
Becomes limitless.
The surrounding darkness transforms
Into countless stars shining in the sky.

- Think about some situation in your life where you feel stuck – a wall you run into again and again, with no way out.

- Sit with your thoughts about this place for a few minutes, attempting to feel yourself slamming into the wall.

- Now begin to pray. Invite God, who is the Place of the world, to be with you in this place. Stuck. Trapped. We call God in as we would call in a rescue squad. We allow our prayer to open a new path in the darkness.

Don't Be Stubborn

לא להתעקש

When you pray
Do not make your prayer fixed [keva],
Rather prayers for supplications
Before the Omnipresent, blessed be He.

Avot 2:13

This is: "Do not make your prayer keva"; the term "keva" connotes "stealing," as it is written (Prov. 22:23): "And rob [kava] the life of those who rob them."

That is, no matter what a person requests, be it livelihood or children or other needs – it is forbidden for him to stubbornly insist and be obstinate in his prayer, that God must fulfill his prayer. For this is a "keva prayer" – he takes the thing by force, by robbing it. Rather, as explained, he is to pray "compassionate pleas and entreaties."

Rebbe Nahman of Breslov, *Likutei Moharan*, part 1, torah 196

Often we make requests of God in our prayer.
Sometimes insignificant, sometimes important.
There are times these requests are truly critical,
We want an answer,
Preferably here and now.
In our difficulty, we insist, we pound on the table.

This stubbornness, this strong-armed approach, in the end it will weaken us.
We miss the opportunity buried in the difficulty:

This difficulty is an opening for movement, for closeness, for conversation.

The Holy Blessed One so desires our prayer.

Problems are not something we need only to solve or to make go away.

They offer an opportunity to invite us to move into a softer space.

They are an opportunity to share, to talk.

Stubbornness limits God,

Insisting: "My way or no way."

If we can let go a bit,

The answer to our prayers can come from a place we can't imagine right now.

We can allow the Holy Blessed One to surprise us.

We can speak to God with soft words,

In language of compassion,

Of supplication,

In conversation with Life.

- We search for something in our prayers that we consistently return to, asking again and again, insisting upon it.
- Find a new way to say this prayer, with softer words, sharing, without any trace of demand. Ask for what is in your heart, but also remain open to the possibility that something good may come from reality as it is.
- Conclude this prayer with words like: "And in the end – I place my spirit in Your hand." Or: "God, I truly want this, but I know that You run the world and I let go and give over my burden to You."

A Melody

ניגון

ה׳ לְהוֹשִׁיעֵנִי וּנְגִנוֹתַי נְנַגֵּן כָּל יְמֵי חַיֵּינוּ עַל בֵּית ה׳.

ישעיהו לח, כ

The Lord [has promised] to save me, and we will play my hymns all the days of our life in the house of the Lord.

Isaiah 38:20

I recall my music at night; I speak with my heart and my spirit searches.

Psalms 77:7

The Holy Blessed One said: I will open for Israel their mouth and tongue with words of Torah so that they can praise My name every day, for if Israel will not be in the world I will have no praise and greatness. For if not for the song and melody that Israel says before Me every day, I would not have created the world. Even Israel, for whom the whole world was created – I only created them for song, as it is said: "This nation I created for Me, my praise they will tell."

Midrash Alfa Beita DeRabbi Akiva, nusḥa alef

The Divine Chamber of Music is a place where hearts open and ascend
Beyond speech, beyond words, moving toward the Infinite.
Between King David's lyre and the ten-stringed harp, the wind blows.
To each movement of the soul, a melody of its own,
A melody that expresses inner murmurings, just like body gestures or hand movements express the voice of the soul.
A melody of thanksgiving, a melody of longing, a melody of pleading,
A melody of joy or a melody of intimacy,
Each one plays different strings of the soul,
Ascends a different musical scale,
Awakens a different spirit within us.

- The world of melody is expansive beyond description and the space here is too limited to really engage with its different realms, so here we will suggest only a preliminary, basic taste.
- Choosing a melody you love, listen to it two or three times with rapt attention. But don't listen only to the beauty of the music, rather listen to how it is an expression of the voice of the soul. Allow the melody to enter your body and to envelop it.
- After listening, pay attention to what was awakened in your soul – what sort of inner movement? Yearning, gratitude, pleadings, praise, and maybe even an inner cry? This awakening can be translated into prayer, or, for a few moments, simply stay in the emotion that arose.

המיית הלב

Call of the Heart

לַמְנַצֵּחַ עַל נְגִינַת לְדָוִד: שִׁמְעָה אֱלֹהִים רִנָּתִי, הַקְשִׁיבָה תְּפִלָּתִי.

תהלים סא, א

For the conductor, with instrumental music, of David.
Hearken, O God, to my request, listen to my prayer.

Psalms 61:1–2

The initial bedrock from which speech grows
Is the voice.
When the voice is born, before words and prior to sentences,
One's desires are already beginning to sprout.
Being revealed is the possibility of the turning to another, of a conversation.

The voice precedes words.
The way the words of the prayer sound becomes their meaning,
Paving for them a path to their destination.
It's as if the melody of the prayer
Lifts the words on its wings,
Whispers between the pages of the prayer book,
Amongst the prayer shawls,
Ascends from the place of prayer to the Holy Ark,
Soars through the windows, out to the boundless skies.

- Sitting in a comfortable, quiet place, begin to make sounds. Primal sounds, basic ones, much like a baby. *Aaaah, Ooooh*. Just a sound, without meaning, without words.

- From these raw sounds move slowly to a melody. Whatever melody comes. The chant of a beloved prayer or the movement of voices together in a more harmonious manner.

- After this experiment of making sounds, choose a section of the prayer book, say it one time as it is, without a melody. Next, say it once again, this time allowing the words to play themselves. It is important not to plan what melody to use, but rather to allow it to rise from within the words themselves.

מחוות הגוף

The Body's Gestures

I come before You
God and God of my ancestors
With a heart broken and down,
Prostrate, humbled, begging and supplicating.
Like a poor man at the door
Sighing and beaten down
Asking, requesting, and begging as a free gift
    and an act of mercy
That You should show me Your wonderful love
    and kindness
And take me out of darkness into the light.

Likutei Tefillot 1:5

Contact
Sivan Har Shefi

My daughter asks for a dance
I touch her lightly, she
Whirls
Like a Tibetan prayer wheel
There are set words
For her beauty
And with tears in my eyes
(Like:
Please God)

Like prayer flags, her hair
In the wind
There are prayers that rise upward
Of themselves

I simply follow with my gaze

פתיחה: ללא מילים
Opening: Wordless

כָּל
עַצְמוֹתַי
תֹּאמַרְנָה
ה'
מִי כָמוֹךָ!

תהלים לה, י

*All
My bones
Shall say,
Lord,
Who is like You!*

Psalms 35:10

My soul yearns and also pines for the courts of the Lord; my heart and my flesh pray fervently to the living God.

Psalms 84:3

Bar Kappara said: To You is bending, to You is leaning, to You is bowing, to You is kneeling, for to You every knee shall bend, every tongue shall swear... and now, our God, we thank You and praise Your glorious name. We bow with all our heart and all our soul. "All my bones shall say Lord who is like You, who saves a poor man from one stronger than he and a poor man and a needy one from one who robs him?" Blessed are You, God of thanksgiving.

Y. Berakhot 1:5

Even before humans knew how to speak, they prayed.
Prayer preceded words,
The body preceded speech.
The body's gestures are the most elemental expression of a person's feelings.
They do not only accompany words and enrich them,
But rather they are a world unto themselves.
The movements of the body are the simplest, most foundational expression of the movements of the soul.
They help us to understand the soul even prior to words.
For example, bowing in gratitude is not a translation of words of gratitude,
Rather it is the body's gesture that holds the feeling of thanksgiving within it.
The standing in the Silent Prayer, the different body movements throughout it,
They are themselves prayer.
The wordless raising of one's hands to the Heaven is a prayer.
We can pray to God
Through the expressions of the body
To let it say what it has to say.
To be like a flickering candle
Like a tree in the forest
Like the ocean's waves.
To be in movement
To be in prayer.
If we listen to our body,
We will know how to perceive the meaning of its different movements.

עמידה
Standing

There are eight things that one who prays must be careful about and do, but if he is pressed, or forced to, or he transgressed and did not do them they do not invalidate [the prayer] and these are: standing and facing the Temple and fixing the body and fixing the clothes and fixing the place and aligning the voice and bending and bowing.

Rambam, *Hilkhot Tefilla UVirkat Kohanim* 5:1

When we are on the level of standing before God alone, then God, out of the love of Israel, may they multiply, also stands before us like we stand before Him.

Rebbe Levi Yitzhak of Berditchev, *Kedushat Levi, Parashat Beshallaḥ*

And this is why the eighteen-blessing prayer is called the Standing Prayer, for that is where the person stands before his Master. And the Kingdom of the Heavens is like the kingdom of the land, like a human king. Anyone who wants to come into the inner court of the king must go first from courtyard to courtyard, and from the courtyard to the hallway, and from the hallway to the hall, and from the hall to the chamber of the king's house. And when he comes before the actual king, then he is in the aspect of standing and not walking. For the essence of the walking he did before was only to arrive at the aspect of standing before the king.

Rebbe Avraham Yehoshua Heschel of Apt, *Ohev Yisrael, Parashat Nitzavim*

The body speaks.
Every movement is sound, every gesture is expression.
If we will look, listen, feel,
We will be able to expand the range of our expression,
To find an inspiring, new channel through which to pray.

The most basic movement of prayer is standing.
Know before Whom you stand.
Standing in prayer expresses steadfastness, standing in presence,
Perhaps even an emphatic demand.
Alternatively we can see it as a willingness to receive, to hear,
Without evading, without turning away.
Standing connects the ground upon which we our feet stand,
The earth from which we came,
To the heavens that our heads reach,
And to which our hearts aspire.

The peak of our communal prayer is called the *Amida*, which means "standing."
In the *Amida* prayer, we stand before God.
It is a prayer that is whispered, a sharing of a secret between us and our Maker.
Let's consider the movements that make up the *Amida*:
Beyond the simple, upright stand,
There are additional movements that give voice to the body
Like the three steps we step back
At the beginning of the prayer,

That have within them hesitation, awe, distance, almost surrender,

And afterward, three decisive steps forward in which we resolve, approach, refuse to yield.

There are also the hands, even they participate in prayer: they strike the chest, they may be outstretched, or dropped at our sides.

And the eyes – where are they turned?

There are different possibilities within Jewish law, and also different tendencies of each and every worshipper.

One possibility: A wordless *Amida*

- Take deep breaths, allowing the body and the mind to quiet and relax, clearing, as much as possible, all words from your head.

- Rise to your feet,
  Take three steps backward,
  Three steps forward,
  And stand – a stand that is prayer.
  Notice the edges of the body,
  The top of the skull and the soles of the feet.
  Sharpen the awareness of the ground upon which you stand,
  To the air above the head.
  When you feel a desire to do so, you can bow, bend the knees,
  Pound the chest,
  Raise your hands.

- Stand until you feel your prayer is complete.
  Take three steps back,
  And sit down.

Another possibility: A prayer of the body

Normally, we activate the body,
We guide it.

This time we will allow it to pray on its own.

- We stand, and let the body lead us,
  To pray with the gestures natural to it.

- We allow the body to surprise us, and to reveal to us the prayer that is stuck inside it.

- It is worthwhile to allow the body to move in ways that are unknown to us, to be in a place lacking in judgment, and to simply experiment…

כריעה

Bowing

בֹּאוּ נִשְׁתַּחֲוֶה וְנִכְרָעָה, נִבְרְכָה לִפְנֵי ה' עֹשֵׂנוּ.

תהלים צה, ו

Come, let us prostrate ourselves and bow;
Let us kneel before the Lord, our Maker.

Psalms 95:6

The sages taught: The term kidda means bowing upon one's face, as it is stated (I Kings 1:16): "Then Batsheva bowed [vatikod] with her face to the ground." Keria means bowing on one's knees, as it is stated (I Kings 8:54): "From kneeling [mikkeroa] upon his knees." Hishtaḥava means bowing with one's hands and knees, as it is stated (Gen. 37:10): "Shall we, I and your mother and your brothers, come and bow down [lehishtaḥavot] to you to the ground?"

Berakhot 34b

In bowing
We attempt to soften the straight line, the upright body.
To bow our head to the One Who is above,
To bend ourselves over,
To remember that we are beneath God,
That abundance comes to us from God's hands.
We curl
Come closer
Touching – not touching.

When we pray we are in movement, almost a dance,
From bending to straightening
From a circle to a line
We bend over and we rise up
A descent for the sake of ascent.
Through our body's movements, we raise the *Shekhina* from the dust.

The *Shulḥan Arukh* details the way in which we are meant to bow in prayer:

One who is praying needs to bend until all the vertebrae in the spine are bent. He should not bow from the hips; the head should not stay straight, rather it should be bent over like a cane.

When bowing, it should be done quickly, and when straightening, one should straighten slowly, raising up the head first, and then the body, so it is not a burden.

Shulḥan Arukh, Oraḥ Ḥayim, Hilkhot Tefilla, siman 113, se'ifim 4, 6

- Practice the directives of the *Shulḥan Arukh* for bowing and straightening at a time separate from your daily prayer.
- Afterward, the next time you pray, attempt to pay special attention to the manner in which you bow and straighten. Pay attention to the vertebrae in your spine, to the bowing of your head, to the speed of your bow, and the moderation of your straightening.
- Let the body's movements be accompanied by the feelings of the soul.

נפילת אפיים

Falling

וַיֹּאמֶר דָּוִד אֶל גָּד צַר לִי מְאֹד נִפְּלָה נָּא בְיַד ה׳ כִּי רַבִּים רַחֲמָיו וּבְיַד אָדָם אַל אֶפֹּלָה.

שמואל ב כד, יד

And David said to Gad, "I am greatly oppressed; let us fall now into the hand of the Lord; for His mercies are great; but into the hand of man let me not fall."

II Samuel 24:14

So I fell down before the Lord the forty days and the forty nights that I had fallen down; because the Lord had said to destroy you.

Deuteronomy 9:25

When one falls on his face, the custom is to lean on the left side. And after one falls on his face, he should raise his head and supplicate a bit while sitting, every place according to its custom; and it is a common custom to say: And we know not what to do.

Shulḥan Arukh, Oraḥ Ḥayim, Hilkhot Nefilat Apayim, siman 131a

We've arrived at the final stretch.
In just a moment our prayer will end.
We stood, we bent, we bowed,
Now is our last chance.
We fall to the feet of the One to whom we've faced in prayer

Weeping, pleading,
Using our last opportunity, as it were,
To ask again before the gates lock.
In the prayer's final chord,
After we've tried to open gates with different keys,
We begin to understand that nothing depends on us
And we know not what to do.
Strengthless, wordless.
What remains is only to fall at the feet of our Sovereign.
We lift our soul upward
Falling into God's outstretched arms
Placing into God's hands our prayers
Our life.

- At the conclusion of the *Amida*, we sit down, lean forward, our head hidden in our left arm, *Nefilat Apayim*.

- We sit quietly for several minutes, without speaking.

- We pray *Nefilat Apayim*: "Have mercy on me, my Lord, for I languish; heal me, my Lord, for my bones shake with terror…. The Lord heeds my plea, the Lord accepts my prayer."

- At the end, we say: "And we know not" and sense ourselves giving over our prayer to God, giving over our body to the fall, letting go.

- We rise with these words: "What we will do."

הידיים בתפילה

Our Hands in Prayer

פֵּרַשְׂתִּי יָדַי אֵלֶיךָ נַפְשִׁי כְּאֶרֶץ עֲיֵפָה לְךָ סֶלָה.

תהלים קמג, ו

I spread out my hands to You; my soul is like a weary land to You forever.

Psalms 143:6

So he was with his hands in faith (Targum Onkelos: spread in prayer) until sunset.

Exodus 17:12

Fixing the body – how is this done? When one stands in prayer, he must align his legs one to the other; and turn his eyes downward, as if he is looking at the ground, and his heart should be facing upward, as if he is standing in Heaven; and he should place his hands on his heart intertwined – right over left. And he should stand like a servant before his master, with fear and awe and dread. And he should not place his hands on his hips.

Rambam, *Hilkhot Tefilla* 5:4

The voice is the voice of Jacob
And the hands?
What do the hands do in prayer?
The hands are raised

The hands accompany our words with movements,
Explaining, beseeching.
The hands spread out above us
The hands dance
The hands clap
Connecting the left and the right,
Moving the air,
The hands rest upon one another
The hands carry the heart to the Heavens
The hands pray.

The raising of hands in prayer
Like Abraham in his time
Like Moshe in the war with Amalek
Like Rabbi Shimon bar Yoḥai in his prayer
Is the giving of power over to the Holy Blessed One.
It is the testimony that all is in God's hands
And with God's strength, our hands act and create in God's world.

- We stand before God in a wordless prayer.
- We move only our hands, as the heart moves us to do.
- We try different movements of the hands: we raise them up, open them to receive abundance, we clap our hands, rest one upon the other, or we lay them at the sides of our body. We allow the hands to express themselves, the prayer concealed within them.

נשימה
Breathing

כֹּל הַנְּשָׁמָה תְּהַלֵּל יָהּ הַלְלוּ יָהּ.

תהלים קנ, ו

Let every soul praise God. Hallelujah!

Psalms 150:6

Rabbi Levi said in the name of Rabbi Ḥanina: For every breath that a person takes they should praise the Creator. What is the reason? "Let every soul (neshama) praise God," let every breath (neshima) praise God.

Genesis Rabba, *Parashat Bereshit, parasha* 14

O Master of the Universe, You are the Primary Cause, and Producer of Results, who irrigates the tree through that spring. That spring is like the soul to the body, in that it gives life to the body.

Petaḥ Eliyahu, *Tikunei Zohar, daf* 17

Often we experience prayer as something separate from us,
A stepping outside of our boundaries: with longing, desire,
    pleas, submission.
But there is a kind of prayer that is simply sitting with what is,

Receiving the abundance
Connecting deeply to what is inside us right now
To the flow of life that beats within us.

We turn our attention to the breath:
Inhale
Exhale
Repeat.
We are in the circle of life that flows within us at every moment
The blood flows
Life flows
Through our breath, vitality constantly flows within.
God sustains us
As if watering trees.
We pay attention to our breath
And accept the Divine abundance
Allowing it to pass through us
Again and again.
We allow the air to enter on the inbreath
And exit on the outbreath
Not trying to reach any place
Not trying to guide our words beyond ourselves
But rather to be
In deep connection.
Soul
Breath
Allowing the Divine flow of life to pass through us
We will be blessed by it.

אנחה

Sighing

יָגַעְתִּי בְּאַנְחָתִי אַשְׂחֶה בְכָל־לַיְלָה מִטָּתִי בְּדִמְעָתִי עַרְשִׂי אַמְסֶה....

I am weary from my sighing; every night I sully my bed; I wet my couch with my tears. My eye is dimmed from anger; it has aged because of all my adversaries. Turn away from me, all you workers of iniquity, for the Lord has hearkened to the voice of my weeping. The Lord has hearkened to my supplication; the Lord has accepted my prayer.

Psalms 6:7–10

See how precious is the sigh and groan of a Jewish person. It provides wholeness [in place] of the lack.... And sighing is the extension of the breath. It corresponds to erekh apayim (patience) – i.e., extended ruaḥ. Therefore, when a person sighs over the lack and extends his ruaḥ, he draws ruaḥ-of-life to that which he is lacking.

Rebbe Nahman of Breslov, *Likutei Moharan*, part 1, torah 8

Prayer is a bridge between where a person is
And the higher will that beats within.
At times it is a bridge that raises us beyond ourselves,
Beyond the here and now, to a place of yearnings,
And at times it is a bridge that descends and prods to the
    deepest depths,
Connecting each one of us to ourselves and our place.
It is this kind of bridge that creates the sigh.

The sigh is a kind of speech, a kind of prayer
A passive prayer
A wordless prayer.
Hiding within it words that aren't said,
Encapsulating in a moment all that there was to say.
I stand facing the gap
Between what I wanted and what is,
Between what I dreamed of and what I have,
And I sigh.

The sigh is an extending of the breath
Breathing deeply into reality
As it is
As I am.
I stand facing the Holy Blessed One
With empty hands
A *schlepper*
Not denying who I am
Releasing the dream
While the dream still beats within me
Sighing from the depths of my broken heart
And God, as it were, sighs along with me.

- When the time is right, sigh from the depths of your heart, without holding back. A deep sigh that fills the body with new breath, bringing spirit into the empty spaces.

Speaking to the Body

דיבור לאיברים

וּמִבְּשָׂרִי אֶחֱזֶה אֱלוֹהַּ.

איוב יט, כו

And from my flesh I see judgment.

Job 19:26

And Hannah, she was speaking in her heart.

I Samuel 1:13

Rabbi Matanya said: I feel indebted to my head, for when I would reach the Modim prayer, it would bow on its own.

Y. Berakhot 2:4

Prayer is wider than the earth and deeper than the seas.
It hovers over the pages of the prayer book
Whispered from one person to the next
Given over through the beats of the heart.
It is revealed through the flow of life
In a state of consciousness, in the quality of speech.
Often we direct our prayer
Toward our God in Heaven

Or perhaps to the God who fills all worlds.
Prayer invites us to direct it internally,
Inward.
From my flesh I saw God
To speak to the body
With enormous mercy
To uncover the light within it
To turn to it, to thank it, to request of it, to entreat it,
To pray through it.

- Sitting quietly for several minutes, relax the body's muscles and breathe deep, conscious breaths.

- Once relaxed, attempt to feel the prayer that is stored in the body. Choose a specific limb to focus on now and open a dialogue with it. Encourage and awaken it to the service of God, to the doing of mitzvot, to pull the body after the heart. For example, you might turn to the hand and speak to it: My hand, my right hand, don't tighten up so much, open up, give charity, reach out. Or, speaking to the heart: My precious heart, I feel your dreams, your pounding. Perhaps you could open up, soften a bit. Why not? Is that so much to ask?

- It is important to give space for the words to arise, as they are, without judgment or cynicism.

קבע ותחנונים

Fixed Prayer and Pleading

You Who are filled with compassion have compassion on us.
Have pity and mercy on our days and our years.
Send the goodness that comes from Your true good.
Merit us to pray truly.
May we recite all our prayers before You with all our heart and our soul.
May we never disdain prayer, which stands at the height of the world.
May our prayer never be routine, but always a plea for compassion,
And may our prayer never appear before us as a burden, Heaven forbid.
In Your vast compassion, help us strengthen, encourage, and fortify ourselves in every way to pray to You with all our heart, truly and properly.
Our Father in Heaven, You know how hard it is
For us to open our mouths to pray.
Our prayers are flawed. In Your great compassion, have pity on us.
Help us redeem our prayers

From the great and bitter exile that has befallen us now because of our many sins.

Have pity and mercy, have pity and compassion

Have pity and save us quickly for the sake of Your name alone

For Your sake and not for our sake.

Open the mouth of a mute such as I.

"God, open my lips and my mouth will speak Your praise."

Prepare my heart. Listen to me.

Help us, You Who are filled with compassion, You Who are in the midst of the praise of Israel,

Help us so that our prayers will always be smooth in our mouths.

Likutei Tefillot, part 2, prayer 1

You are the Voice

Michal Govrin

You are the voice and we are Your speech
You are the voice and we are Your letters
You are the voice and we are the tongue that
    pronounced
And we are the lips that expressed
And we are the teeth that shaped Your words

See how we are carved with breath
How the hands are inscribed
That will rest at the end of the day
On the table between the knife and the bread

See Your words rise up in us from the world
See Your voice calling out from our lives
See us inscribing You day and night
And may these words be on Your tongue
Do not forget

פתיחה: חידוש בתפילה
Opening: Renewal in Prayer

Rabbi Eliezer says: One who makes his prayer fixed, his prayer does not constitute pleading.

Mishna Berakhot 4:4

What does fixed mean?

Rabbi Yaakov bar Idi said that Rabbi Oshaya said: Anyone for whom his prayer is like a burden on him.

And the rabbis say: This means anyone who does not recite [prayer] in the language of supplication.

Rabba and Rav Yosef both said: This means anyone unable to introduce a new element [into their prayer].

Berakhot 29b

Sometimes our prayer can become regular, a fixed prayer,
And it comes to feel like an unbearable burden.
There are those who get bored, yawn, begin to count the pages yet to go.
There are those who stare out into space, mumble the words, waiting for the end.

The printed, set prayer book
Can cause our prayer to become rote.
But if we smooth its pages, ponder the spaces between the words,
We will sense how each prayer was written in a moment of inspiration, of Divine guidance.
Each word in the prayer book is a word that comes from the heart
And reaches the heart of the world.
Each of its words was born in a moment of connection, rising up from within the heart.

In order to transform the words of our prayer from fixed words
To words that are alive, vibrating, calling,
We must say them from the heart, we must get to the heart of them.
We can sing before God a new song,
Look at the ancient words with new eyes,
As we see them in this moment,
And to say them in a fresh, clear way.
This allows us to discover the power that lies in the fixed movement, in the repetition,
In the submission,
To awaken the mercy in the regularity, the pleadings.

ממלמול לפנייה
From Mumbling to Facing

Turn to Me and be saved, all the ends of the earth;
For I am God, and there is no other.

Isaiah 45:22

I called to You because You shall answer me, God.
Bend Your ear to me; hear my saying.

Psalms 17:6

It is told of Rabbi Levi Yitzchak of Berditchev
That he once noticed that the prayer leader in his synagogue was hoarse.
He asked the prayer leader how this had happened, and the man answered him: "I prayed before the congregation."
Rabbi Levi Yitzchak replied to him: "You are right. The prayer leader who prays before the congregation, his voice becomes hoarse. But the one who prays before the Living God, his voice does not."

It is not by chance that one of God's many names is:
El, "To."
The One Who turns To.
There is One To Whom we can turn.

At times our words are detached.
Or, as Rebbe Nahman of Breslov calls them: Words from the nape.

Words that don't face anyone,
Faceless words.

One of the most important things in prayer
Is paying attention, and refining our listening:
What is my purpose right now? To Whom am I speaking?
    Toward Whom am I facing?
This is the most basic meaning of intention in prayer:
To transform mumbling into facing.
To turn the words toward their destination
To aim them in the right direction.
Beyond addressing God, throughout the prayer book we vary
    the recipient of our words
Such that, for example, in *Pesukei DeZimra*, the initial psalms
    we recite at the beginning of our morning prayer, we move
    from a calling out to the entire word:
"Give thanks to the Lord, call out in God's name; make God's
    deeds known among the people."
To a plea addressed to God:
"You, Lord, do not withhold Your mercies from me."
And next, turning to the soul:
"My soul, praise the Lord."

The central prayer of *Keriat Shema*, the Reading of the *Shema*, can be read as a public declaration, that God is One. And, alternatively, it is possible to read it as a quiet statement to myself, to listen to the secret of existence whispering from within reality: God is One.

To each verse a different address, a different melody.
Don't make your prayer fixed.

One possibility: In a *ḥavura* (group)

- As we sit together in a circle, one person opens and shares something. Next this speaker turns to someone specific who has been chosen to be the receiver of the words, calling this person by name and directing what was just said specifically to this one listener. Pay attention to what may have changed.

- We may continue by journaling: Everyone can visualize God listening to our prayers right now. We tell God what manner of listening we need in order for us to talk. We write down anything that arises, addressing our words to God.

- Later, when praying our regular prayer, we try to feel that same quality of directing our words to a specific destination rather than into empty space.

Another possibility: With a *ḥavruta* (study partner)

- Two friends sit together while one shares something. The speaker requests the attention of the listener in a very specific manner, stating directly what is needed of them as far as their body position, eye contact, whether they should say anything, whether they should nod…

- It is worthwhile to hold on to the memory of what it felt like to be really heard, and when praying about something, to try to feel this kind of listening to our words, to notice where our words are directed, and whether they manage to move beyond the boundaries of our own space.

A third possibility: Alone or in a ḥavura

- We choose a single Psalm from the *Pesukei DeZimra* or a blessing from the blessings of *Shema*. We read the Psalm or the blessing and focus our attention on the different things or people being addressed. Write on the side of each verse who is being addressed, and add stage directions: how to say it, whom to face, how to stand. When actually praying, we turn our attention to the different addressees.

- When we pray in a ḥavura we can decide ahead of time to divide tasks and to say the Psalm in such a way that will help us feel the transformation from mumbling to turning.

- So, for example, in the Psalm *Ashrei Yoshvei Beitekha*:

- We begin by turning to God: "Praiseworthy are those who dwell in Your house, may they always praise You, Selah." And move on to a request in the third person that is perhaps directed toward those praying alongside of us: "God is great and exceedingly lauded, God's greatness is beyond investigation." Toward the end we turn inward: "My mouth will declare the praise of God," and to those praying with us: "We will bless God from this time and forever, Hallelujah!"

העלאת העולמות
Elevating the Worlds

One should lower his head a little so that his eyes will be down to the ground and he should imagine himself as if he were standing in the Holy Temple and in his heart he should direct himself upward toward the heavens.

Shulhan Arukh, Oraḥ Ḥayim 95

"And he dreamed, and behold there was a ladder" (Gen. 28:2) – this is prayer. "Set on the ground" – for people pray on the ground, which is the Shekhina, and it reaches the Heavens, which is the Holy Blessed One.

Zohar, part 3, 306b

We pour out our prayer and we rise up to a world of whole reality in ultimate perfection, and then our inner world becomes truly whole in complete perfection, and our consciousness is filled with joy, and the same weight with which our inner conviction affects reality, of which our inner self is also part, pushes the whole world to the side of merit.

Rabbi Avraham Yitzhak HaKohen Kook, *Olat Re'iya, Inyenei Tefilla* 7

One of the greatest challenges we face when praying is the length of the prayer service:
"What, I have to say *all* of this?"
We can look at the prayer
Not like a walk down a straight path toward the ever-furthering horizon.
Rather as a ride in an elevator, where on each floor that we reach,
We find before our eyes a completely new world, surprising and different.
A ride in an elevator that elevates us to worlds from which our reality can be seen in a whole new light.
An elevator that brings us to the heart of the world, to its innermost chamber.
A prayer in which we not only recite words, but we sense that we are part of a living event, dynamic and stirring, in which each page of the prayer book holds within it a gateway to another world, another existence.
Our world isn't only the one we see spread before us, but it is built as one world on top of another, a room inside a room, higher and higher.
Prayer is meant to elevate us from chamber to chamber, to skip between the worlds, to rise above the here and now.
Each part of the prayer takes us to a different world,
Like moving from room to room in a museum, like riding in an elevator.

In prayer, we are part of a live event:
Passing from world to world, from room to room, from level to level.
The view changes throughout our prayer. The screen rises on a new setting,
Everything shifts: the sights, the sounds, the smells, the colors.

- As we begin to pray, we can imagine that we are entering into an elevator. We are not simply reciting the words of the prayer, but rather we are lifting them up to the world in which they belong.
- We begin going up in the elevator and step out on the first floor, where we find the first sections of our prayer, the Morning Blessings and the Sacrifices, which focus on our actions in this world, on our hands doing, our body awakening. On our most basic level of existence: opening the unseeing eyes, straightening the bent stature. Raising the material world, our animal soul, higher.
- Ascending to the second floor, we find a more picturesque world, the world of *Pesukei DeZimra*. A world of joy over the entirety of creation, of the poetry of the natural world, of the song of birds, of praise and gratitude.
- The elevator continues to ascend and we move into the world of angels, the *Serafim* and the *Ofanim*. We hear them whispering through their wings, calling to one another, "Holy Holy Holy." A world of holiness, of God's love washing over us from above, of all of creation becoming one.
- And from here on to the next floor, that of the *Amida*: a world of closeness, of oneness, of the direct emanation of God, an intimacy woven in whispers. We rise up and look out at the visionary landscape, at the Heavenly Jerusalem.
- Now we can descend from the penthouse all the way down to the parking level, to bring the vision down into the reality of our life…

The Daily Prayer

תפילת התמיד

Rabbi Yehoshua ben Levi said:
The prayers were instituted based on the daily offerings.

Berakhot 26b

May it be Your will, Lord our God and God of our ancestors, that this recitation be considered, accepted, and favored before You as if we had offered the daily sacrifice at its appointed time and place, according to its laws.

From the Morning Prayers

Rising in the morning
Waking like a lion
Hurrying to report for service of the Divine
Even without desire, even without strength
Even without focus
Making my prayer regular
Obedient
I bow my head
Like a soldier in God's army
As a servant before a lord
Day after day
Prayer after prayer
"You shall offer one lamb in the morning
And the other lamb you shall offer at twilight."

> Choose one of the three daily prayers and approach it with the mindset of a servant serving the master.
>
> With this prayer we make a special effort to begin on time, to concentrate on the words, to pray as part of a community of worshippers. We pray this prayer like a sacrifice going up on the altar of God, not pausing to consider our own private feelings. Even if not all of the words of the prayer are clear, we recite them as they are, understanding that the very recitation of them has power. They will pull out of us the inner movement of obedience and subordination. We notice our posture in this prayer, how we hold our body.

לחדש בה דבר

Making It New

Rabbi Eliezer says: One who makes his prayer fixed, his prayer does not constitute pleading.

Mishna Berakhot 4:4

What does fixed mean?
Rabba and Rav Yosef both said: This means anyone unable to introduce a new element [into their prayer].

Berakhot 29b

To introduce a new element – into his request. And this is the meaning of "fixed" – yesterday is like today is like tomorrow.

Rashi ad loc.

And we must understand this, for if it is so, you lock the door of prayer for most of the world who do not know how to put new things in their prayer, and it is enough [work] for them just to mean the words... but the wonder and the feeling of the heart is always new, so that even if one cannot add something new it is still not called fixed. And from this there is a great learning for those who come to pray with intensity of feeling and wonder in their prayer.

Rebbe Shmuel Bornshtein of Sochatchov, *Shem MiShmuel, Parashat Va'ethanan* 5678

The written prayer is a fixed prayer.
We must make it new
To bring the ancient words inside,
To say them again – alive, fresh, renewed.
To speak to God with an open heart, with warmth,
With wonder and emotion.
To reveal the movement from which the words were born
Before they were expressed,
Before they were written.

- We choose one of the blessings of the prayer book.
  The evening prayer, *Maariv Aravim*, for example.
  We read it, feel it, listen to it, try to get a sense of it:
  From what emotion were these ancient, holy words written?
  What was the experience of its composers,
  The sages, the members of the Great Assembly?
  We attempt to enter that same emotion,
  To be moved as they were.
  But this time – from our own place.

- Taking a pen and a piece of paper, we write a new version of the prayer,
  Personal, yet following the same framework –
  "Blessed are You" in the beginning, "Blessed are You" at the end.
  Afterward, when we return to the prayer book,
  And we say the blessing of *Maariv Aravim*
  We find that our personal intention joins together with the ancient words
  And renews something in them.

תפילה בלשון תחנונים
Prayer as Supplication

א. לעורר את דיבורי הלב
A. Arousing the Words of the Heart

The act of speaking is very effective for spiritually rousing a person. Even if it seems to him that he has not feelings, when he speaks many inspirational words, supplications, entreaties, and the like – the very act of speaking is the concept of revealing and rousing his heart and soul for God. This is as in "My soul came forth when he spoke" (Song. 5:6). The speaking is itself a revelation of the soul and the heart. Thus, sometimes, as a result of a great deal of speaking, even when it is without any feeling, one's heart and soul are afterward greatly inspired. The principle is that the act of speaking in itself has great power.

Rebbe Nahman of Breslov, *Likutei Moharan*, part 2, torah 98

Behold our eyes see that it is impossible for there to be one thought every day like the day before, or the one before that. So in prayer, one should also renew it the way he sees fit in his mind. And this needs an expansive consciousness and strong intention that one's heart and mouth and thought should be aligned, agreeing on one thing, as is known, which is not true if one prays in a fixed way like yesterday or the day before, with the regular language, the head bowing on its own at Modim, and the heart not with him.

Rebbe Yaakov Yosef of Polonne, *Toledot Yaakov Yosef, Ekev*, 3

When praying we want to truly speak
To merit speech that opens hearts.
Speech that creates a reality.
Speech that forms worlds.

The world was created with speech.
Therefore, one who becomes accustomed to speaking with the Creator
Can reach a place where new words are born,
Words that go beyond my limited and regular self,
Remaining open to discover.

The words of the heart are like a muscle.
We must warm them up slowly,
Soften them,
Awaken them.

We let the words of prayer work on us.
We allow the heart's intent, hidden in the words, to awaken us.
We sense the invisible bridge
Drawn between the ancient words
And our time, into our lives.

One possibility:

- Choose a section of the prayer book (for example, one blessing of the *Amida*) and read it through ten times, in a different manner each time. Use changing rhythms, varying tones, with different emphases. The purpose of this repetition is to search for the manner of reading that will create a new perspective on the words such that the heart will open when reading them, and an authentic, new prayer will be created as they are said.

Another possibility: With a ḥavruta

- Before beginning to pray, we choose a partner,
  We sit next to one another.
  When we arrive to the recitation of *Keriat Shema*,
  One whispers into the ear of the other:
  And you should love the Lord, your God
  With all your heart
  With all your soul
  With all your being.
  Continue like this, until the end of the first section of *Shema*.

- Reading the prayer out loud, along with saying it directly to a friend,
  Can open the heart
  And awaken love.
  Talking about love creates love between us.
  We manifest our love for God,
  We experience it, we marvel at it.

ב. בוא אל התיבה

B. World of Words

For on the face of it, it is hard to understand why we have to pray when God knows [all our] thoughts. However, this is because words are the vessels of bounty, through which we receive the influx of bounty. As it is written: "And bless you as He said to you" (Deut. 1:11) – i.e., the influx of bounty is in accordance with the speech. If the words, the vessels of bounty, are perfect and in fullness, then we can receive abundant bounty in them.

Rebbe Nahman of Breslov, *Likutei Moharan*, part 1, *torah* 34

One should put out his speech before God, the Blessed One, with love and awe and repentance and joy, and put all of his strength and life force in the words that come out of his lips, as it is explained in the holy books about the verse (on Noah): "Come you and all your household to the teiva (a word that means both "ark" and "word").… The main thing is speak words of Torah and prayer with all of your strength, and then cleave to the Infinite light, Blessed Be, which dwells in the letters.

Rebbe Yisrael Baal Shem Tov, *Mekor Mayim Ḥayim, Parashat Noaḥ*

The world was created with words.
Let there be light – and there was light.
Words are the materials the world is made of
Its building blocks.

The word is not only a symbol agreed upon for this thing or that thing
Rather each word has a life of its own.
It creates reality
It has substance
Like a face expressing a person's inner essence, the word
Unifies form and content.
Each and every word
Has its own light
The energy stored within it
Its own feeling.
Each word is like a bud growing and blossoming.
The flat, printed script stands out and becomes a word, three-dimensional
Calling to us: Enter in, create a world.

- During our prayer, we choose a specific section and when reading its words, we don't just say them and move on, but we give substance and reality to each and every word. We should not look at each word as two-dimensional, just ink on a page, but rather as three-dimensional.

- Imagine the word as a living entity, possessing texture, voice, and color. In our mind's eye, we see the word standing in the air, independent and separate, possessing a light all its own. After this contemplation, we send it on its way.

טוב מעט

A Little Bit Is Good

Better few supplications with concentration than much without concentration.

Shulhan Arukh, Oraḥ Ḥayim 1:4

I also heard that [Rebbe Nahman] spoke about prayer with a certain ordinary person who had great difficulty praying. The Rebbe gave him advice and told him to think to himself that he needs to pray only till Barukh SheAmar, since perhaps in this incarnation he has to rectify only this section of the service. It is possible that already in a previous incarnation he prayed the rest of the service with proper concentration, so that now, in this incarnation, all he has to pray with proper concentration is this section until Barukh SheAmar. Consequently, he should invest all his energy into this modest amount, praying with proper concentration… because a small amount can be said with proper concentration, and then afterward, a little more, etc.

Rebbe Nahman of Breslov, *Likutei Moharan*, part 2, *torah* 121

Prayer has a countless number of gates,
Words, verses, supplications, and songs.
This plethora of gates allows each worshipper to find their own portion
To open the gate that fits the moment
To illuminate the soul through today's prayer.

We can imagine the prayer book as a kind of menu:
We enter the synagogue
Sit down, contemplate the prayer book.
Certain words capture our attention
Prayers that call to us specifically today
A song of the day.
Just as we don't eat all of the food that appears on the menu,
No one expects us to pray with the same strength
Everything that appears in the prayer book.
Each day and what it brings
Each day and its choices.

- In our daily prayers we say many words, and we aren't able to pause on each one and pray with proper concentration for the entire length of our prayer. The set, ordered recitation of the words is also meaningful; the very saying of the words of the prayer influences us and the worlds above us.

- Nevertheless, during the recitation of the entirety of the prayers it is worthwhile to stop from time to time on a verse that expresses our feeling in the moment, to repeat it several times, to pause on a section that awakens us today, that expresses the yearning of the heart, today.

תפילה בציבור

Communal Prayer

May it be Your will,
My God and God of my fathers,
That Jews should meet and bond with each
 other every day
To serve You and fear You.
May every individual speak with his friend
About the fear of Heaven
And inspire his friend to serve You and fear You.
May we remind each other
Strengthen each other
And inform each other of Your truth, Your
 faithfulness,
Your greatness, and Your goodness that fill the
 entire world
So that the "direct light" and the "reflected light"
 will constantly be drawn down through us.
May the Holy Temple be built and completed
Through us constantly
Every day, every moment, and every hour.
May all the holy lights shine in our hearts
So that we will truly awaken and turn to You
 with a whole heart…
And may the verse be realized in us:

"Those who hear God spoke together,
  each man to his neighbor,
And God took heed and heard;
And a book of remembrance was written before Him
For those who fear Hashem and cherish His name.
May the words of my mouth and mediation of my heart be pleasing before You. God, my rock and my redeemer."
Amen and amen.

Likutei Tefillot, part 1, prayer 124

Everyone Needs
Chana Friedman Uhlman

Everyone needs someone to pray for him.
Someone whose lips will utter his name
In faith and hope and life, to revive someone
Else and everyone needs a heart on which to place hands
In faith and blessing, and everyone needs someone else
And needs to go out and go in and mainly to go beyond
And forget himself and for a bit to go in and for a bit to be
Someone else for an hour, for a day, for a cry.
To be someone else.
Everyone needs to stand before his God
And to cry out enough, no more
Let him be, let him be, he's pure gold,
He is a precious gem, he is Your
Son, Your one and only,
Give him good, visible and revealed, give him also,
Give him also, the ability to pray.
Help him pray
For someone else.

פתיחה: תפילה כאחד
Opening: Praying as One

The Rebbe also said that it may be impossible to go through the entire service with proper devotion. Still, each person can say a small portion with true feeling.

We see this all the time. One person might have deep feelings while saying the Ketoret, and another may pray best during the Pesukei DeZimra, etc....

This is as it is brought in the Tikunei Zohar (tikun 18): There are masters of the hands and masters of the feet. There is a transcendental counterpart of the human body, and each of its limbs corresponds to a portion of the service. Each person is also associated with a particular limb. When he comes to the part of the service pertaining to his limb, he is aroused to great devotion.

Rebbe Nahman of Breslov, *Siḥot HaRan*, 75

With each soul that is added and increases the gathering of Jews, the House of Prayer is greatly increased and expanded.

For now, when one more soul is added to the gathering, many, many other, new permutations are made, increasing their number exponentially.

Rebbe Nahman of Breslov, *Likutei Moharan*, part 2, torah 8

In communal prayer we come together to stand before God
Facing our lives, facing our existence.

In communal prayer, I am not alone, I don't need to hold
   everything by myself.
I have partners. A sacred community.
We are like a philharmonic orchestra:
One plays the flute, another the piano, yet another the drums,
Each person playing their own part.
At times the violin rests and the piano plays boldly
And then they switch.
There are many roles:
One prays, another calls out to the *Kohanim*,
Another collects the prayer books.
We are like a single body
With one whose strength is in the hands, another in the legs,
Another in the ears, and another in the eyes,
Each one focusing on a different part, each one opening a
   different gate.

And even I, perhaps in a different time in my life, once merited
   to say with intention
What now is lost to me.
Not everything rests on my shoulders
Here and now
I am not alone
My existence began before me
And my friends are here, surrounding me
Playing together
Focusing together
Praying together
To the Master of the World.

תפילת הדורות
Prayer Through the Generations

The kindnesses of the Lord I shall sing forever; to generation after generation I shall make known Your faithfulness, with my mouth.

Psalms 89:2

That he may turn the heart of the fathers back through the children, and the heart of the children back through their fathers.

Malachi 3:24

When telling a story, the main question is where to begin
How to spin together the story's threads
Each possible starting point weaves a different story.
We are also asked this question when telling our own life's story:
Where do I begin?
I can begin my story from the moment I woke up this morning, from this past year,
Or from when I was born, or when my parents were born.
Or I might look back even further to previous generations from whom I've evolved, generation after generation,
Extending my days back to my ancestors and my ancestors' ancestors,
Drawing them into my story, to my descendants and the descendants of my descendants.
To pray as a part of a continuous prayer carried from generation to generation
A communal prayer, a prayer of our people.
To open my heart to the world: to its pain, to its hopes,

To give an immeasurable breadth of context to life.
I connect my prayer to the prayer of the generations, to the stirring that arises, generation to generation.
Moving among holy places – from the resting place of Rabbi Shimon bar Yoḥai to the tomb of *Raḥel Imenu*
From the Cave of the Patriarchs to the Temple Mount.
I hear the prayer that is rising up to me from the depths of the Earth
Calling out the forefathers and foremothers, to the righteous ones of each generation,
That they should pray with me, that I should pray with them
That my prayer be included with theirs.

- Beginning with the following words, we write our own prayer:
  "My God and the God of my ancestors
  God of Abraham, Isaac, and Jacob
  God of Sarah, Rebecca, Rachel, and Leah."
  Continuing, we write down, by name, all of our ancestors known to us – God of my great-grandfather and great-grandmother, grandfather and grandmother, father and mother, going back as far as possible to previous generations.
- After mentioning their names, we continue and write the prayer that arises inside us right now, our ancestors present in it.
- We can also look forward to younger generations, mentioning them by name: God of my children, my grandchildren, my great-grandchildren… and write a prayer in their merit and with their strength.

ואהבת לרעך כמוך
Love Your Friend as Yourself

הֲרֵינִי מְקַבֵּל עָלַי מִצְוַת עֲשֵׂה שֶׁל וְאָהַבְתָּ לְרֵעֲךָ כָּמוֹךָ...

Behold I accept upon myself the positive commandment of "And you should love your fellow as yourself," and I hereby love every one of the Jewish people as myself and my essence, and I call on my mouth to pray before the King of the kings of kings, the Holy Blessed One.

From the prayer book, *Nusaḥ Sepharad*

Before a person sets his prayer in the synagogue, from the "Binding of Isaac" and on, he should accept on himself the commandment of "And you should love your fellow as yourself," and have in mind to love every Jew as himself, for through this, his prayer will include all the prayers of Israel and can rise up high and give fruit.

Rabbi Hayim Vital, Introduction to *Shaar HaKavanot*

Communal prayer is not an individual's prayer said amongst others.
Rather it has a character and quality all its own.
The key offering of communal prayer
Is the ability to open our hearts to see ourselves
Not as private people
But rather as part of an entire organism
To release us from the hold we have on ourselves, on our needs.

It is not by chance that our prayer is worded in the plural
Because prayer's main tenant is the inner ability to rise
Above our solitude
And be part of a whole, one with the community.
The first gate of connection to the community of which we are part
Is to fill our heart with love.

- When praying in a *ḥavura*
  We begin by opening our hearts:
  After our initial greetings, we sit together,
  Around a large table or in a circle,
  In a way that everyone can see one another.
  We look at one another,
  Into each others' eyes,
  We hold intention.

- Only then do we say together:
  "I hereby accept upon myself the commandment of the Creator to love my friend as myself."
  After this statement we pause a bit.
  Opening our hearts, we look around the room, and notice those sitting with us,
  Knowing that they also have a prayer, a desire, a yearning.

- It is worthwhile to listen:
  What feelings arise up in us when we sit in a *ḥavura*?
  What different kind of focus does this partnership awaken in us,
  What new prayer is born?

תפילת הציבור
The Community's Prayer

אֲשֶׁר יַחְדָּו נַמְתִּיק סוֹד, בְּבֵית אֱלֹהִים נְהַלֵּךְ בְּרָגֶשׁ.

תהלים נה, טו

That together we would devise counsel;
In the house of God we would walk with a multitude.

Psalms 55:15

For in mind and intellect people's consciousness is not equal. Therefore from the side of mind and intellect even when they are together they do not become one. A community which is as one person is only from the side of the heart, for all of Israel has only one heart toward their Father in Heaven.

Rebbe Shmuel Bornshtein of Sochatchov, *Shem MiShmuel, Parashat Va'ethanan*

In community prayer, in a *ḥavura* of worshippers,
We come together to God,
We step out of our isolation, our separation,
And connect.
We move from ten individuals, to a *minyan*, a quorum of prayer.
From twenty legs standing one next to the other – to ten
　　hearts beating together.
In our prayers for one another, we raise the level of love that
　　exists among us,
The responsibility and the connection.
This wondrous connection between us is what allows us to
　　open our hearts
And to pray for one another.

- When praying in a *ḥavura*, we can invite, at the prayer's outset, anyone who would like to ask for the help of the group:
  To express a request or mention the name of another who is in need of prayer, to give their own name to the group, and the entire group together can repeat the name out loud and pray.

- Another possibility is to have everyone to sit together in a circle and everyone writes down their own requests.
  All of these notes are then collected and placed in the middle of the circle.
  Each one then reaches out a hand, randomly chooses one of the notes, and reads out the request written before him with focus.
  Sometimes you might receive your own prayer.
  Sometimes you might receive a prayer similar to your own, like a sort of wink from Above.
  And at times, only once we have begun praying we may find that the prayer of another, that had at first seemed distant and strange to us, has unearthed in us a new desire, revealing how the root of all prayer is one.
  This is what it means: "One who prays for a friend is answered first" – answered with a new prayer.

- Afterward, in the midst of our prayer, we will recall the same request, and pray about it in the appropriate places.

- The knowledge that someone in the room is praying for me, while I am praying for another,
  ties us together with invisible strings,
  brings us closer.

שליח ציבור
Sheliaḥ Tzibur, an Emissary of Prayer

Know, too, that someone who is capable of making these melodies,
That is, gathering the good points that are to be found in each Jew,
Even a Jewish sinner,
This person can lead the communal prayers.
For one who leads the communal prayers is called the emissary of the people;
And this emissary must be sent by all the people;
That is, he must gather every good point that is to be found in each of the congregants.
All these good points are merged in him,
So that when he stands to pray, it is with all this good.
This is the meaning of sheliaḥ tzibur.
Thus, he must have within him this exalted aspect,
As a result of which all the points are drawn to him and become merged within him.

Rebbe Nahman of Breslov, *Likutei Moharan*, part 1, torah 282

The Hebrew phrase for prayer leader, *sheliaḥ tzibur*, means literally, "emissary of the assembly," and as the name implies, the *sheliaḥ tzibur* is just that: an emissary for the prayer of the whole.
Receiving strength from the community of worshippers,
The *sheliaḥ tzibur* becomes bound to their souls,
Fixing to their prayer a mouth and wings.

From within the *sheliaḥ tzibur's* own inner awakening
    to prayer,
The hidden prayer in the heart of each worshipper is stirred
    and illuminated.
The prayer leader lights the fire, awakening desire and shining
    light.
The *sheliaḥ tzibur's* special perspective on the congregation
Allows the unique prayers of each worshipper to be felt
As their prayers are brought to light.

Like a magnet, the *sheliaḥ tzibur* draws out the prayers, collects them together, and raises them to their destination. Hidden prayers emerge from their silent hiding, and bind themselves together to become a melody.

- Before stepping up to the podium as the *sheliaḥ tzibur*, we try to sense who is present, honing our ability to listen, and deepening our inner contemplation: What is the prayer hidden deep within them? What desires are stirring in the air? We feel the responsibility and the mission that has been placed on our shoulders, and notice the expectation of those gathered, waiting for someone to lead their prayer.

- When praying together as a group, we can ordain the *sheliaḥ tzibur* before beginning our prayer; we can form a circle and place our hands on the head of the *sheliaḥ tzibur* as if to say: Take us with you, guide us with your prayer. Anyone who would like can share with the *sheliaḥ tzibur* something to include while leading the prayer.

תפילת הכלל
The Prayer of the Collective

To understand "receiving the face of the Shekhina": For our rabbis of blessed memory said, "Make your ear hear what comes out of your mouth," meaning the Collective spirit of Israel which is called You… and they said that a person has no obligation in prayer, except to hear and contemplate what You – the Collective of Israel – bring out of Your mouth,… and all of Israel is interconnected with one another; what one is missing can be found in another, and when they all come together as one they are a whole body.

Rebbe Shneur Zalman of Liadi, the Alter Rebbe, *Likutei Torah*, Song of Songs 2:2

"O God, how numerous are my tormentors, many [rise up on me]" (Ps. 3:2). Every person, depending on his soul and his service [of God], such is the suffering of his experiences. One person suffers experiences from his children or from his father or from a neighbor. Another person is on a greater level than he; he experiences suffering from distant neighbors. Another is still greater; he experiences suffering from the entire city. And one who is very great, he experiences suffering from the entire world. Now each person, by virtue of the suffering, carries on himself those people from whom he suffers. For when he experiences suffering from them, he carries them on himself.

Rebbe Nahman of Breslov, *Likutei Moharan*, part 1, torah 170

Who am I?
At times, I am only me,
And my prayer is personal.
And at times, I am able to expand myself,
To become one of the congregation,
To become a receiver for the prayer that surrounds me,
Prayer that bursts from the lips and hearts of many.
In such prayer I am only a mouthpiece, an emissary of the
 Congregation of Israel,
And so I must first listen to the voices that surround me,
To the prayer ascending from the House of Prayer.
To the unique bonds being created by the community of
 worshippers,
To be a channel for the troubles of others, for their hope, for
 their joy,
A mouthpiece for the glory of the many and varied shades of
 the tribes of Israel, each one asking to be heard.

- Prior to beginning to pray, we pause quietly for several minutes, opening our hearts to sense and to hear the specific frequency that is buzzing in the moment.

- We allow our "I" to soften and to expand, to become one with the surrounding souls, to merge with the being that is called *Knesset Yisrael*, the Congregation of Israel, to open our hearts to what is happening in the world, near and far: to the joys of our neighbors, our community, our entire people; or, God forbid, to the individual or communal pain that is felt when there is a terrorist incident, an accident, or another kind of tragedy. To absorb the prayer that rises from the widening circles around me, like ripples spreading out and expanding beyond me.

- As we open our mouth to begin to pray, we tell our ears the hidden prayer that arose while we listened.

תפילה על השכינה
Prayer for the *Shekhina*

"But You made him slightly wanting from God, and with glory and majesty You crown him" (Ps. 8:6). Behold, it is known that whatever a person lacks, whether spiritually or physically – that want is in the Shekhina…. But when a person knows this, that the want is above and below, he will certainly feel great sorrow and sadness, and so will not be able to worship God with joy. He will therefore have to answer for himself: "What am I, and what is my life? For the King Himself informs me of His want. Is there any greater glory then this?" This brings him to great joy.

Rebbe Nahman of Breslov, *Likutei Moharan*, part 1, torah 89

And Isaac prayed to God opposite his wife, etc. It is known that when some trouble or suffering comes to a person, Heaven forbid, then he should be wise and understand in his mind that surely there is a great pain for the holy Shekhina, so to speak. "For in all their troubles, He was troubled" (Is. 63:9), so to speak. Therefore when a straight person prepares his heart to pray to God about something, his main intention and will in his prayer should be for the fulfilling of the lack that the Shekhina has from this, so to speak.

Rebbe Avraham Yehoshua Heschel of Apt, *Ohev Yisrael, Parashat Toledot*

Standing in Prayer
With empty hands
An awaiting heart
Telling of my troubles, my difficulties, my failings
The longing
For the lack that cries out from my life.
Slowly, slowly the heart breaks
Opening to the pain that envelops the world
Listening to the suffering, the hardships surrounding
Softening
Feeling the pain of the *Shekhina* in exile
Telling me of Her lack, of Her sorrow.

- Choosing some feeling of lack that is difficult and troubling right now, we detail this lack and describe it fully.
- Next, we turn to the Holy Blessed One, and we say: "I know that this issue isn't really only my personal problem, rather a problem of the whole world, and also Your problem." (For example, "I am not the only single person in the world, there are many other singles like me, and also You, God, lack a home, but it hurts me that the world is imperfect." Or, "I am not the only person who angers easily, there is so much rage in this world, and so many natural disasters filled with fury.")
- We pray about the lacking in the world and in the *Shekhina*. We ask and we beg. It is important not to make the strength of our prayer artificial, but rather a genuine expression of how we can pray about this now.
- Once we have prayed for the world and for the *Shekhina*, we can also make our own personal request.

עצות לתפילה בציבור
Advice for Praying in Community

Quiet Moments

When praying in community it is important to notice the moments of quiet that arise spontaneously, or as a community to choose to add them in: a moment of silence after the prayer *Yishtabaḥ*, a minute of quiet after the Kaddish prayer.

Quiet without pretense, a quiet of repose, of supplication.

To allow for space between the words, to stop the consistent flow, to allow for transition, waiting.

Responsive Prayer

In prayer it is valuable to seek as many as possible opportunities for cooperation between the congregation and the *sheliaḥ tzibur*. For example, the prayer *Barukh SheAmar* can be said as a prayer of call and response: the *sheliaḥ tzibur* says one part and the congregation answers.

Blessed is the One Who spoke and brought the world into existence.

Blessed is God.

Blessed is the One Whose words are deeds.

Blessed is the One Who decrees and fulfills.

Where to Stand?

It is important to consider the question of where I should stand in the synagogue, to choose my place in the synagogue in a conscious way. To choose the right place for myself considering the physical make-up of the synagogue and in relation to those praying with me.

Singing Together

In communal prayer it is a challenge to sing together. To open my ears to the singing around me and to become a part of it. To sing and to listen at the same time. The advice is to be sure that my voice does not exceed the voices of those that I hear around me.

תפילות משנים קדמוניות

Prayers of Ancient Days

Grant us salvation in Your great mercy
That we may merit in our prayer
To bind ourselves, individually and as a community,
With all beings and with the holy souls of those who sleep in the dust.
May we awaken them with our prayer
So they will pray together with us
As it is written: "Awake and sing, you who sleep in the dust."
Then, as we connect our words of prayer to those who sleep in the dust,
As a whole, and with each one in particular,
Let us merit to awaken in our prayer
All the parts of our souls that have come into an incarnation and been rectified.
Let us also merit to awaken
All the holy souls of the Righteous Ones who sleep in the dust,
The holy ones in the earth,
So that they will pray together with us
And in their merit may our prayers be heard always

And You shall heed our voice and listen to our outcry
And have compassion on us for their sake, not for ours,
As it is written: "As for the holy ones in the earth and as for the mighty ones, all my desires are fulfilled because of them."

Likutei Tefillot, part 1, torah 55

Ancient Song
Zelda

A very ancient song
Wakened me to life
When it banished humility from me
With the lips of kings.
A song of a generation
That went silent
Ages and ages ago
Awakened me to life.

פתיחה: ירושת אבות
Opening: Inheritance of Our Ancestors

יְהִי ה׳ אֱלֹהֵינוּ עִמָּנוּ
כַּאֲשֶׁר הָיָה עִם אֲבֹתֵינוּ
אַל יַעַזְבֵנוּ וְאַל יִטְּשֵׁנוּ

מלכים א, ח, נז

May the Lord our God be with us
As He was with our ancestors;
Let Him not leave us, nor forsake us.

I Kings 8:57

Our holy forefathers and foremothers left us a grand inheritance
An inheritance stained with tears
An heirloom hewn from the heart.
Abraham, Isaac, and Jacob,
Sarah, Rebecca, Rachel, and Leah,
Moshe Rabbenu, Hannah, Hezekiah, King David,
And all those who prayed throughout the generations
Left for us prayers
That open the gates of heaven
Pierce the abyss
In precise, concentrated words.
A kind of capsule
A secret hidden within
Offering us
To take up the craft of our ancestors
To use their prayers as a mold for our own
To pour into them new prayers
And to open our mouths in prayer.

תפילה קצרה

A Short Prayer

אֵל
נָא
רְפָא
נָא
לָהּ

במדבר יב יג

God
Please
Heal
Her
Please

Numbers 12:13

A most basic prayer of Moshe Rabbenu for his sister Miriam.
A brief, concentrated prayer
Carrying within it the DNA
Of the components of the prayer of request.
The precise choice of words creates a pure and powerful prayer.
A prayer consisting of a mere five words that we may use
    as a basic template for the prayer that is the secret of
    constriction.

אֵל	To – the Addressee, using one of God's many names
נָא	Please – a word of request
רְפָא	Heal – the content of the request
נָא	Please – a powerful repetition of the word of request
לָהּ	Her – the subject of the request.

Onto this basic template we can cast our personal prayer, when the need arises to focus our prayer, to concentrate our soul's petition.

אֵל	Any form of appeal that arises: Merciful One, Hashem, Father, Shekhina. The more varied our collection of names is, the more accurately the name we choose can fit the content of the request.
נָא	Any expression of petition that is natural to us: please, בבקשה, *por favor*, if You would…
רְפָא	The content of our request: Grant success, Redeem, Bring joy, Answer.
נָא	A repetition, intensifying, stressing, and pleading; not just a request, but rather the act of requesting itself.
לָהּ	The subject of our prayer, the person or the thing about which we are praying: Myself. My father. My people. My sister. My friend. My wife. My husband. My children.

קטונתי

I Have Become Small

קָטֹנְתִּי מִכֹּל הַחֲסָדִים וּמִכָּל הָאֱמֶת אֲשֶׁר עָשִׂיתָ אֶת עַבְדֶּךָ...

And Jacob said, "O God of my father Abraham and God of my father Isaac, the Lord, who said to me, 'Return to your land and to your birthplace, and I will do good to you.' I have become small from all the kindnesses and from all the truth that You have done for Your servant, for with my staff I crossed this Jordan, and now I have become two camps. Now deliver me from the hand of my brother, from the hand of Esau, for I am afraid of him, lest he come and strike me, [and strike] a mother with children. And You said, 'I will surely do good with you, and I will make your seed [as numerous] as the sand of the sea, which cannot be counted because of multitude.'"

Genesis 32:10–13

Our father Jacob passes through the Jordan River for the second time in his life
and realizes in wonderment how much water has flowed through since then.
He turns this contemplation on the vicissitudes of his life into a tender prayer.
Jacob's prayer can serve as a formula
With which we give expression to the sense of smallness that sometimes overwhelms us in the face of the loving grace that is extended to us,
As well as the request for salvation and rescue that we are still so in need of, despite the great abundance and love we've received.
The request or the cry that rises from within an expression of gratitude is softer, not demanding. It is given over not only to the lack, but rather balances between the feeling of abundance and the gratitude for it, and the difficulties and the challenges.

Jacob's prayer has four parts that can be used to help us create a formula for our personal prayer:

1. Calling by name:
   "God of my father": Explicitly listing the names of one's father and mother and grandfather and grandmother.
   "God who says to me": We attempt to identify and to verbalize what God is saying to me right now, as to my destiny in the world or of the Divine will being revealed to me.

2. Acknowledging the good:
   This section of the prayer we say in the exact language of the verse: "I have become small from all the kindnesses and from all the truth that You have done for Your servant"
   "For… And now…" We describe the original place we were once in, as opposed to our present situation; we describe the mercies that God has lavished upon us, the abundance that envelops us, and we detail why we feel unworthy, small in relation to what we've received.

3. A precise and well-reasoned request:
   "Save me…" We ask God for something for which we still feel we need God's salvation. We repeat the request several times. Please, please…

4. Justifying the request:
   "And you said..." We explain the request, why we are worthy of this redemption, this salvation.

We write down our personal prayer according to this formula and once we've done so we pray our prayer before God. It can happen that between the composing of the payer and its recitation, our prayer can change.

מי שענה הוא יעננו
The One Who Answered Will Answer Us

מִי שֶׁעָנָה לְאַבְרָהָם אָבִינוּ בְּהַר הַמּוֹרִיָּה הוּא יַעֲנֵנוּ...

He Who answered our father Abraham on Mount Moriah, may He answer us.

He Who answered his son Isaac when he was bound atop the altar, may He answer us.

He Who answered Jacob in Beit El, may He answer us.

He Who answered Joseph in the prison, may He answer us.

He Who answered our forefathers at the Sea of Reeds, may He answer us.

He Who answered Moses in Horeb, may He answer us.

He Who answered Aaron when he offered the censer, may He answer us.

He Who answered Pinhas when he arose from amid the congregation, may He answer us.

He Who answered Joshua in Gilgal, may He answer us.

He Who answered all the righteous, the devout, the wholesome, and the upright, may He answer us.

From the *Selihot* Prayers

In times of trouble
We turn with our struggle to God
And strengthen ourselves:
We count on our past experience,
On answered prayers.
The One Who answered –
Will answer us.
We turn to God:
You answer our whisper
Just as You answered –
Answer me.

- We say the above prayer as it is written.
  And add two lines:
  The One Who answered us in ... will answer us.
  The One Who answered us when ... will answer us.
  Examples from Jewish history in both the distant and recent past abound. For example:
  The One Who answered us in Jerusalem during the Six Day War will answer us.
  The One Who answered when scuds fell on Tel Aviv in the Gulf War will answer us.

- We add two additional lines of personal prayer
  The One Who answered me in ... will answer me.
  The One Who answered me when ... will answer me.
  We look at our own personal history:
  When and where did I cry out to God?
  When and where were my prayers answered?
  So for example:
  The One Who answered me when I cried of loneliness when I left home will answer me.
  The One Who answered when I lost my job and was broke will answer me.
  The One Who answered me when my mother lay sick in the hospital will answer me.

- We finish with the closing sentence:
  The One Who answered all of the righteous ones and all of the devoted ones and all of the innocent and upright ones will answer us.

- We can also write a prayer as a couple, about things we have experienced together over the years and through so many life events, places where we witnessed God's salvation. And we can recite the prayer together, with one saying "The One Who…" and the other responding "will answer us." A prayer of call and response, where one calls out and the other answers, is a prayer that reflects itself – the hope of an answer from God.

תפילת חזקיהו
Hezekiah's Prayer

אָנָּה ה׳ זְכָר־נָא אֵת אֲשֶׁר הִתְהַלַּכְתִּי לְפָנֶיךָ בֶּאֱמֶת וּבְלֵבָב שָׁלֵם וְהַטּוֹב בְּעֵינֶיךָ עָשִׂיתִי...

In those days Hezekiah became critically ill, when Isaiah the son of Amotz the prophet came to him, and said to him, "So has the Lord said, 'Give orders to your household, for you are going to die and you shall not live.'" And he turned his face toward the wall and prayed to the Lord, saying, "Please, O Lord, remember now, how I walked before You truly and wholeheartedly, and I did what is good in Your eyes." And Hezekiah wept profusely... And the word of the Lord came to him, saying... "I have heard your prayer; I have seen your tears. Behold I shall heal you."

II Kings 20:1–5

King Hezekiah faces harsh and difficult news.
He turns his face to the wall, faces the feeling of having nowhere to go,
Faces mortality,
He prays
And cries.
He mentions himself to God
His whole heart, his goodness
And sobs deeply, holding within his wordless cry all the pain and the hurt.
God hears his prayer
God sees his tear
And promises:
I will heal you.

Hezekiah's prayer can serve as a capsule for prayer in extreme situations, when we face difficult news or great doubt.

- Turning our face to the wall, real or metaphorical, we lay out before God all the things we have done until now, inviting the Divine to remember the good in us, all we have done truthfully and with a whole heart.

- The request itself, to cancel the evil decree,
  We do not mention explicitly.
  But rather we hide it
  In tears, silence, or crying out wordlessly.

Psalms

תהלים

A person should endeavor to find himself within all the psalms
And within all the supplications, entreaties, penitential prayers, and the like.
And easily, simply, without any sophistication,
He can find himself within all the supplications and entreaties,
And especially in the psalms, which were composed on behalf of the Jewish people
For each and every one personally.

Rebbe Nahman of Breslov, *Likutei Moharan*, part 2, torah 101.

On the topic of the recitation of Psalms: Rebbe Nahman told a person with whom he spoke that the main thing in reciting Psalms is to say all of them referring to oneself, finding oneself in each and every chapter.

Rebbe Nahman of Breslov, *Likutei Moharan*, part 2, torah 125

A poem touches the reader's heart
When it transcends the poet's own experience,
Releasing the experience of one
To the great wind
That carries the poem beyond.

King David, the poet of the Psalms,
Bound to his royalty,
The Divine Spirit beating within him,
Playing his harp.
His words have been whispered ever since
Through the generations
Tears absorbed in a book
Lips moving.

To read the Book of Psalms
And to feel the Divine inspiration from which the words were carved
To see the face looking out at me from within the verses
To sense the life-force of the words
And through them, my own vitality.

- Opening the book of Psalms randomly, we choose one that appears on the page we've opened to.

- We say the Psalm four times in a row, and while doing so we see where we are in relation to the ancient words, verse after verse.

- If the words fit where I am at right now, and describe me well, I can add the word "I" to the beginning of them. For example, "I implored You with all of my heart." "I contemplated Your ways." This isn't solely King David speaking, it's also me.

- If the words do not describe my current situation, if they are far from me or feel strange to me, I can transform them into a prayer. For example, "At midnight I will rise to give thanks to Your name" can be transformed to "You know, Master of the World, how much I would like to get up to pray in the middle of the night, and how hard this is for me to do. Perhaps You can help me and I will merit to rise and give thanks to Your name."

- A third possibility is that the words do not move me at all or speak to me in this moment, and so I leave them, and see them as a kind of mirror reflecting where I am really at right now.

הקשבה למענה

Listening for a Response

Master of the World
Master of the World
Speak on behalf of a mute such as I
Open my mouth and let my words shine
I will hope in God, I will seek His face
I will ask Him to respond
"A man prepares his heart but God provides the answer of the tongue"
"God, open my lips and my mouth will speak Your praise"
God, open my lips so I will be able to express my speech to You
And tell You everything that is in my heart. "I will speak and gain relief"
I will speak, no matter what I have gone through.
I will stand firm and beseech, pray, and plead
Before You Who are filled with compassion
You Who hear the prayer of every mouth
Perhaps God will yield to me
And I will no longer suffer any losses from now on, Heaven forbid.

Likutei Tefillot, part 2, prayer 35

In My Descent
Sivan Har Shefi

And when I went down the valley, the mountains were accompanying me
To my right and to my left, like the bride's parents
And like the Sabbath angels
And singing to me:
I will not fear.

And when I returned from the ritual bath
In the distant expanse
There the end of summer thorns were gleaming
Like the stars of dawn

And the world would quiet itself in my descent
And behind me, without turning my head, were the mountains
My prayer was like a mound of white rocks
And fog like a cotton field moved thick and concealed from me
Who I was until just then.

And when I went down with open hands to my house
Down beneath,
I was weightless
And a simple light came toward me
To receive me.

פתיחה: פנים אל פנים
Opening: Face to Face

נַפְשֵׁנוּ חִכְּתָה לַה׳ עֶזְרֵנוּ וּמָגִנֵּנוּ הוּא...

Our soul waits for the Lord, our Helper and our Shield.
For our heart will rejoice in Him, because we hoped in His holy name.

Psalms 33:20–21

Now the spirit entered me when He spoke to me, and it stood me on my feet, and I heard what was being spoken to me.

Ezekiel 2:2

Know! Connecting and cleaving to God is mainly through prayer. For prayer is a gate through which we can enter into [the presence of] God and it is from there that we can know God. This is because prayer is the aspect of Malkhut, as it is written (Ps. 109:4), "But I am prayer." And prayer [tefilla] connotes connectedness, as it is written (Gen. 30:8), "With bonds of [naftulei] God have I been bound [niftalti]," which is rendered as connoting connectedness.

Rebbe Nahman of Breslov, *Likutei Moharan*, part 2, torah 84

Prayer is a meeting
A connecting of Heaven and Earth
A search for Your face, Your presence
For speech.
And as in any meeting
We are not alone
There is someone who is listening to us
Someone who is turning to us
Who shines their face at us.
If we remember this
We can redeem prayer from its solitude
And merit, perhaps,
To hear the voice
That speaks to us
And answers.

מענה לשון
An Answer in Words

אוֹחִילָה לָאֵל אֲחַלֶּה פָנָיו...

I shall await the Lord, I shall entreat His favor.
I shall ask Him to grant my tongue eloquence.
In the midst of the congregated nation I shall sing of His strength;
I shall burst out in joyous melodies for His works.
The thoughts in man's heart are his to arrange,
But the tongue's eloquence comes from the Lord.
O Lord, open my lips,
So that my mouth may declare Your praise.

From the High Holy Days Prayers

For it is impossible to pray unless the Holy One, blessed be He, opens the chambers of the heart, and opens the lips in prayer. Without this there is no true reality of prayer at all.

Rebbe Tzaddik HaKohen of Lublin, *Resisei Laila* 20

For the essence of mercy is in the heart. Then words flow from the Supernal Heart.

Rebbe Nahman of Breslov, *Likutei Moharan*, part 1, torah 20

Occasionally the prayer book serves as a kind of anthology of prayers
Offering words to the heart's stirring that I do not know how to express.
And at times when I have no words, my prayer comes from the Heavens, offered as a gift:
The heart's feelings lie waiting within me, seeking a way out, seeking expression
When suddenly the words become clear, I am able release them
The words themselves are a response to my prayer.

The very ability to give words to the expressions of my heart is in itself a kindness
My very speech is a sign from God that my prayer has been received.
The prayer that leaves my lips bears witness to the connection between us.
Like a good conversation, where the quality of listening gives birth to the speech
If my prayer is flowing – then there is One Who is listening to it and attending its birth.
The moment of a prayer's birth is a moment of wonder,
The One Who gave humans a mouth
Opened my lips
And behold, here is my prayer before You.

- We sit in silence for several minutes, listening intently to the stirrings of the heart, without speaking.
- Noticing what inner desire arises, we sit with it.
- We seek and request the right words to express our desire.
- When the words are revealed to us, we open with a prayer: initially with the words of the verse "Lord, open my lips, so my mouth can tell of Your glory" and continuing with the words that emerge and become clear, through the answer I received, in the prayer that arose.

נשיאת כפיים
The Priestly Blessing

"Behold he is standing behind our wall" – behind the walls of synagogues and houses of study, "looking in from the windows" – from between the shoulders of the priests, "peeking in from the cracks" – from between the fingers of the priests, "My beloved answered and said to me" – what did he say to me? "May God bless and protect you."

Song of Songs Rabba, *parasha* 5

We pray the morning prayers.
We praise with the verses of *Pesukei DeZimra*,
We express wonder, we are moved through the blessings
  preceding *Shem*a,
We find Oneness in the reading of the *Shema*,
We focus through the *Amida*.

Now we reach the stage of the prayer in which we change
  direction:
Until now we thought, focused,
Strove to imagine, talked.
Now we listen,
Open to blessing,
To receiving a response.
Now God is the speaker
And we listen and receive the blessing,
Giving it over to the different parts of our life.

We enter our prayer shawl, enveloped
With ourselves, with our children,
Eyes closed and heart open wide.
Before the Holy Ark the priests stand,
Facing us,
And they speak to us in God's name:

May the Lord bless you and watch over you.
May the Lord make His face shine unto you and grant you
  favor.
May the Lord lift up His face toward you and grant you peace.
We open to receive the blessing,
Filling our heart with it.

קריאת התורה
Torah Reading, Calling

The entirety of the Torah is names of the Holy One, blessed be He.

From Ramban's Introduction to the Commentary on the Torah

*And this is the meaning of mikra, the reading or calling
   of the Torah,
Like a person who calls a friend to come,
So too, through the letters of the Torah one calls the Holy
   Blessed One
To be revealed below,
And as our rabbis of blessed memory taught:
The Holy Blessed One calls
And learns opposite him.*

Rebbe Shneur Zalman of Liadi, the Alter Rebbe, *Torah Or Mishpatim* 77, 3

"I have strayed like a lost lamb; seek out Your servant..." (Ps. 119:176). But God's way is to call the person immediately when He sees him straying from the way of the intellect. He calls to him to turn back. And [God] calls to each person according to his aspect. To one He calls with a hint, and to another with an actual call. There is also one whom He tramples down and punishes, and that is his call. For the Torah calls to them, "Fools, how long will you love being misled?" (Prov. 1:22). And the Torah is God Himself, who calls to them and seeks them, that they should return to Him.

Rebbe Nahman of Breslov, *Likutei Moharan*, part 1, torah 206

The entire Torah is names of God.
In Hebrew the word *kore* means both "read" and "call."
When we read the Torah, we are not only reading, but also
 calling God by name,
And God calls back.
During the Torah reading we are passive,
We don't say anything
We don't respond at all
Only listen.
From within the congregation one rises,
The Torah reader,
And calls God in the name of us all,
And the Holy Blessed One calls back in response.

Torah reading is the time in our prayer when we stop for a
 moment,
We cease saying our part in the prayer,
And listen to what the Holy Blessed One has to tell us this
 week.
This is not the time for ideas about the weekly reading,
Or for studying the Torah's commentaries,
Rather for the Torah reading, for the calling:
A time for listening to Divine speech
Bursting from the Torah.

We direct our hearts to listen to the reading,
To awaken, to evoke the ancient words,
To transform the reading to a calling,
To hear the Torah calling to us.

One possibility:

- During the Torah reading, we come close to the reader, watching and listening closely. We may close our eyes and allow the Torah's words to envelop us. We can listen to the reading as if we are listening to someone with whom we are in conversation, who is speaking directly to us.

Another possibility: With a *ḥavruta*

- Sitting together with a friend, we choose a section from the weekly Torah reading, and have one read the section to the other, word for word, relating the words directly to the other.

- Upon finishing the reading, the reader turns to the listener and asks – Do you hear?

Hearing Is Responding

שומע כעונה

The sheliaḥ tzibur must connect all the souls praying with him and raise them up, and awaken their heart at the time of prayer, with a great awakening for repentance.

Rebbe Kalonymus Kalman Halevi Epstein, *Maor VaShemesh, Parashat Shemini*

At times the repetition of the *Amida* seems a bit superfluous to us, somewhat boring.
The *sheliaḥ tzibur* repeats the prayer,
Reciting nineteen blessings word for word,
And we answer Amen.
We can see the repetition of the prayer as an opportunity
To experience something different in our prayer,
A bit like riding a train.
Somebody takes me to the place I want to go
There is a pleasant freedom in this
Somebody else is praying for me
And I simply answer: Amen.

The very same prayer that we prayed on our own,
We now pray again –
This time with our ears,
Listening,
Absorbing,
Agreeing.
By virtue of our involvement, both the listener and the speaker unite for a moment,
The mouth and the ear become one.
The prayer leader lifts all of our prayers
This is our chance to give the leader the permission and the strength to do so
To give wings to our prayer.

One possibility:

- During the repetition of the *Amida*, we listen closely to the *sheliaḥ tzibur*, recognizing that each and every word being said is being said in our name, for us.

- In the saying of "Amen" at the end of each blessing, we can have the intention of giving permission to each and every blessing, sending it on its way through the channel of the of the *sheliaḥ tzibur*'s repetition.

Another possibility:

- During a different prayer (for example, during the recitation of *Pesukei DeZimra*) we can sit by another worshipper and listen to them as they pray, allowing this person to lead us and carry our prayer for us.

מניעות בתפילה
Disturbances in Prayer

You Who support the fallen, answer us on the day we call.
You Who support the fallen, rescue us.
You Who support the fallen, save us from all of our troubles.
Please look upon our poverty and support our battles.
You know how difficult the Side of Evil has made our simple service of God,
And only You know how much heaviness and difficulty, how many obstacles and interruptions, the Side of Evil applies.
Making matters troublesome, setting up obstacles and impediments,
So that I will not engage in any of the holy matters, great or small, that I wish to undertake.
This is particularly hard and difficult regarding prayer,
Because, due to my many sins, I cannot open my mouth in prayer and I cannot gather the strength to control my thoughts.
My thoughts wander into words of vanity, into evil, foreign ideas, into desires and fantasies, into so many extraneous types of thought not at all related to my words of prayer,
Until my thoughts are so deeply separated from my words, that for the most part I have no idea what I am saying.
Woe to me! Woe to me!
What shall I say? How shall I speak? How can I justify myself?

Help me, from now on, at any rate, so that throughout the day
And in particular at times of prayer I will overcome all of the foreign thoughts that come to confuse me.
May I not turn my heart to them at all.
Instead, may I invest all of the thoughts in my heart and mind into my words of prayer.
May I connect my thoughts to the words of prayer with a firm and strong bond.
You Who are filled with compassion, help me so that I will invest all of my powers into the words of prayer and totally dedicate my soul and body when I pray.
May my prayer not be like a burden to me, Heaven forbid.
May I toil with all of my strength and with every sort of true counsel to truly pray to You.
In Your mighty compassion and kindness, accept my yearning, my efforts, and my travails as I pray,
As if I had brought You sacrifices and incense offerings to solicit Your favor.
Help me and save me. Strengthen me and bolster me constantly,
So that I will pray to You with the true intent of my heart, with the joy and goodness of my heart,
Without any crookedness in my heart at all.

Likutei Tefillot, part 2, prayer 58

Sought

Admiel Kosman

Sought is a quiet place where the soul may rest.
For a few minutes only.
Sought is a place to plant my feet.
For a few minutes only.
Sought is a flower, a leaf, a stalk, a bush,
That will not rise up
And fold up when she will come.
For a few minutes only.

Sought is just one word, clean,
Pleasant, and warm, to be used as a bench
A shelter, for some girl,
For my kin, a dovelike girl, my soul
That left the ark,
For a few moments, in the morning hours,
And since then has not found a resting place for her foot,
    anywhere.

פתיחה: עבודה שבלב
Opening: Service of the Heart

"To love the Lord your God and to serve Him with all your heart" (Deut. 11:13). What is the service of the heart? Say it is prayer.

Taanit 2a

The working of the heart is like the working of a field. You should not plant amongst the thorns and stones. Rather the beginning of your work should be to clear out the stones, loosen the clumps of earth and separate the pieces, and plow the face of the land to remove all thorns and weeds. If you have done all of these, and prepared the earth to be ready to receive the seeds you will plant, then raise your eyes to Heaven and it will bring down the first rains and the last ones in their time, the land will give its crop and you shall eat its produce. And if you do thus to your field from which comes forth only the life of your body, why would you not do this for your heart from which comes the life of your soul?

Rabbi Yaakov Tzvi Mecklenburg, Introduction to the Siddur *Tefillat Yisrael*

At times prayer is hard work
A real struggle
Almost a Sisyphean effort
To break down walls of alienation, of disconnection,
Of emptiness and distraction.
Our thoughts wander
Time is pressing.
So many obstacles
So many curtains that detach and distance
So many contradictions.
So difficult
To be able go inside
To trust
To connect to my core
To mean what I say
To say a single word
Of truth.

העלאת מחשבות זרות
Raising Up Stray Thoughts

For man is required to believe that the world is filled with His blessed glory, and there is no place empty of Him, and all man's thoughts have within them the reality of God, and every thought has a complete stature. And when, while engaging in prayer, there arises in one's thoughts an evil foreign thought, it comes to him in order to be fixed and raised up.

Rebbe Yisrael Baal Shem Tov, *Keter Shem Tov* 39

We all know the feeling
Of standing in prayer when thoughts arise,
Sometimes bad thoughts, or annoying, or embarrassing ones,
Sometimes just strange, disconnected thoughts.
What can we do?
We can relate to these thoughts not as a disturbance,
But rather as voices, as desires, as sparks gathering around our prayer,
Asking to cling to me, wanting me to be a mouthpiece for them,
To fix them, to raise them to their source,
To transform them into prayer.
Don't be afraid. Don't fight. Don't push back.
Just turn, redirect the energy upward.
Turn the distractions into prayer, alienation into closeness.

- When a thought arises in prayer that is unconnected, bothersome, or strange, notice it, consider its source, what it might be coming to fix, and how we can transform it into prayer.

- For example: If while praying a troubling thought comes to mind about livelihood or money, ask:
  What is this troubling thought?
  Why am I troubled by money?
  Perhaps for the welfare of my spouse and my children?
  And on top of this we can also ask:
  What is this desire in me to see to the welfare of my family?
  And through this it might become clear that there is actually no disturbance or stray thought, but rather a deep prayer:
  Please God, I am asking of You, give me the necessary means,
  Help me make it possible for my family to free themselves from external constraints,
  So that they are able to do what their heart truly desires,
  So they are able to freely express their own voice in this world.
  And so in the merit of this stray thought, I find myself praying out of love for my spouse and my children,
  Asking for their light to shine, for their voice to be heard.

לחדור מבעד למסך
Penetrating the Barrier

Behold, it is known that "the wicked walk round and round" (Psalms 2:9). For the Other Side surrounds holiness…. And should his spirit be aroused to return to God, he finds it very difficult to pray and speak before God words. For they surround him from every side, each one according to his circumstance…. Therefore all the words and prayers that he does speak are incapable of breaking through the dividing partitions and screens, so as to ascend Above. They remain below, beneath the screens, until he is deserving and honestly returns, and speaks words that are worthy of being received – with fear and love from the depth of the heart, with great arousal. Then, the illuminating words break through all the dividing partitions and screens, and elevate together with them all the words which until now remained below…

The intelligent person who understands should pray all his days that once in his life he should merit to properly speak one word of truth before God.

Rebbe Nahman of Breslov, *Likutei Moharan*, part 1, torah 112

Sometimes, when standing to pray,
One hears voices from inside,
Feelings, memories, experiences,
That arise within and arouse opposition,
Cause doubt,
And together form a sealed, opaque, and diffuse barrier.
A barrier that does not allow one to sense reality in its full power
And pray freely.
Let's not deny these disturbances.
On the contrary – let's acknowledge them, give them an image and a clear voice.

- First we look closely at the barrier surrounding us during prayer: What is it made of? What does it look like?

- Now we move on and ask: What is the voice coming from the barrier? What are the voices hindering our prayer saying?

- We listen to them, formulate them in clear words,
  For example:
  "I don't mean these words seriously."
  "I don't believe God is really hearing me."
  "I'm not in the right space to really pray."
  "I'm sick of myself."
  Once you've formulated the thoughts into clear words,
  Say them out loud. Don't hold back.
  Imagine these voices as actual people,
  Surrounding you and preventing you from reaching your destination,
  Your prayer.

- From this confrontation we practice paving a way through the voices.

- Perhaps, by standing up to these voices, some point of truth will emerge.
  Perhaps you'll sense how in some way, despite everything, you really are serious.
  You might actually find that you really believe.
  You will discover which prayer you actually have the headspace for, right here and now.

You might, for just a moment, trust yourself.
Perhaps the right words will succeed to break through the barriers and your prayer will rise out of them.

Recipe for a *ḥavura*:

- Each one of the participants, in turn, tells someone else what they would like to be able to say, and what prevents them from to doing so, what dims their voice.

- The *ḥavura* takes upon itself to turn the challenge into something concrete:
  The one praying stands up and begins to walk, all the while voicing their prayer out loud.
  Three "disturbers" surround, repeating out loud the bothersome thoughts:
  The first: "Come on, you aren't saying this completely honestly. You don't really mean what you're saying."
  The second: "You don't really think God is hearing you, right?"
  The third: "Forget it, anyhow you're not focused now."
  Repeat this, again and again.

- The presence of the obstacles and the disturbing voices in all their might creates inside us a deep commitment to overcome them,
  To reach an inner point of truth,
  From which one fitting, truthful word to God can break through.

צהר תעשה לתיבה
Shine Light on the Word

Now the main thing is: In his prayers, supplications, and requests – even if he finds it impossible to recite any word of prayer and supplication because of the intense darkness and confusion which surrounds him, very much from every side, he should still try to at least say what he says with truth, no matter how low its level. Thus, for example, he should say "God help me" with truth, even if he cannot say it with the appropriate fervor and arousal. He should nevertheless say the words as truthfully as he can, and through the true word, he will merit to see the openings within the darkness, and as a result be worthy of coming out of the darkness into the light so as to pray as he should.

Rebbe Nahman of Breslov, *Likutei Moharan*, part 1, torah 112

There are times when our words are surrounded by shells.
We can't seem to form words that come from the heart.
We are afraid to open our heart. Lest we get hurt. Lest we be ashamed.
We fear being too vulnerable, being seen.
We say a lot of words, but they fall flat.

Open speech is the secret of life.
Its mysteries infuse all aspects of our lives.
No word is ever lost.
In the end, all prayers will reach their destination.
All words await their hour, accumulating within us
Until their time comes
And from the depth of our hearts a true word bursts forth,
Breaking through all of the barriers, all the shells with which we've confined ourselves.
Paving a path for all the words that lay within us.
Like a stone with no one to turn it.
The word of prayer, the word that was blocked and enclosed in a shell,
Suddenly shines.
The light of truth shines on it.
Through true speech we can cleave to God, whose stamp is truth.
We can truly live our lives.
True speech opens the channel for prayer and forms the essence of speech.

- When our prayer is "stuck," the advice to break through the barriers is to say the most basic words, from wherever we are at in the moment. To identify what kind of speech is the most fitting right now: words of request or of longing, of distance or pain, of anger or despair.

- We say true words. We distill the exact words that we can stand behind in this moment. Without being afraid to say what is in our heart, even if it is only partial or unclear and even if the content of our words speaks of difficulty and distance. For example:
"It is hard for me to speak. I feel like I haven't been able to talk to You for a while now." "It's hard for me to pray. I don't really believe that anyone is listening to me." "I am full of anger and disappointment and so I am pulling away from You."

- Despite the distance, our honesty and open heart can light up the way, mark the starting point, reveal the openings in the darkness of silence, and bring us closer.

תפילה דרך הצדיק
Praying Through the *Tzaddik*

And give into the hearts of all the righteous ones, those whom I mentioned before you, and those hidden righteous ones who existed in every generation whose names I did not merit to know, that they should – together as one – protect us and pray for good for us before Your seat of glory, that You should have mercy and compassion on us, and put in our hearts to return to You in truth. Remove from us our heart of stone and give us a heart of flesh, and bring us back in complete repentance before You. And we should merit to walk in the path of the righteous, and let our portion be with them in the coming world in the Garden of Eden, and let us not enter with shame before You.

From the prayer after the recitation of *Shemot HaTzaddikim*

The Holy Blessed One desires the prayers of the righteous, for through prayer the righteous one cleaves to the Blessed Creator, and this is the pleasure of God when the righteous one rises up and cleaves to Him…. And the main life force of the righteous one is through prayer, through which he cleaves the Holy Creator.

Rebbe Elimelekh of Lizhensk, *Noam Elimelekh, Vayeḥi*

There are days on which my prayers are stuck
They can't come out
They can't rise up
Something is off.
I look about for someone to help
Through whom I can connect
Like a hot spot where there's no connection
Like cables to jumpstart a dead battery.
I look for a *tzaddik*, a righteous person,
A master of prayer,
And turn for help.
There is someone who understands more than I,
Someone who is an expert in opening the gates,
In revealing the channels.
I can entrust the *tzaddik* with my prayers
Trust the *tzaddik* to pray them for me,
To open for me the gates of prayer.

- During prayer we look around, scan the synagogue, seeking someone who seems to know how to pray, by whom the gates appear open, through whom we would like to send our prayer.
- We imagine our prayer being sent through this person and rising up through their open gate.

ה' מתפלל
God Praying

And with Your great compassion, have compassion on us and pray for us Yourself. Awaken with Your simple compassion Your greater compassion and let the verse that is written be fulfilled: "And with great compassion I will gather them." For You know, Hashem our God, that there is no one who can stand for us, who can awaken compassion for us at this time, for we have become very far from You, as You know, and there is no one who can awaken compassion on us besides You Yourself, our Father, our King. "Please pray for us, and let us live and not die, and the land should not be forsaken."

Rebbe Nahman of Breslov, *Likutei Moharan*, part 1, torah 112

Sometimes we are discouraged from praying, we lose faith in
 the possibility of prayer,
Everything seems blocked.
We have no trust in words, in ourselves,
We feel exiled, distant.
There is no one to awaken compassion for us.
From within our despair
We can reveal a new opening, a surprising one,
And ask God to pray for us,
To give words to our inner scream,
To have compassion on us in our exile.

- We stand before God in prayer. We open with these words: Please God, please pray for me… and begin requesting in detail what we'd like God to pray for us.
- We conclude with these words: Because You are the Master of Prayer and the Source of Compassion.

עבודת ההתבודדות

Hitbodedut:
Private Prayer from the Heart

"Come, my beloved. Let us go out to the field;
Let us stay overnight in the villages. Let us arise
   to the vineyards;
Let us see if the grapevine has flowered,
If the tiny grapes have developed,
If the pomegranates have lost their flowers.
There will I give you my love."
Master of the World, help me always engage in a
   great deal of *hitbodedut*.
May I accustom myself to go out every day to
   the fields, among the trees, grasses, and all of
   the vegetation of the field.
There may I engage in *hitbodedut* and a
   great deal of conversation – that is,
      prayer – between myself and You, my Maker,
Expressing everything that is in my heart.
May all of the vegetation of the field, all of the
   grasses, trees, and plants, be aroused to greet
   me.
May they all rise up and invest their strength
   and vitality in my words of conversation and
   prayer.

Until my prayer and conversation may reach the ultimate perfection with the aid of the plants of the field,
So that all of them, with all of their might, vitality, and spirit, reaching up to their supernal root,
All will be incorporated into my prayer.
As a result, may I open my heart
And engage in a great deal of prayer, pleading, and holy conversation before You.
You, who are filled with vast compassion,
May I pour forth all of my conversation before You
Until I will pour out my heart like water before Your countenance, God,
And lift my hands to You on behalf of my soul and the souls of my children and infants.

Likutei Tefillot, part 2, torah 11

Good for a Man
Zalman Shazar

It is good for a man to be once on his own.
No book, no friend, no community, not a soul,
Just him with his heart, with the heart all alone,
It is good for a man to be once on his own.
And it's good he should leave behind all he has found,
No house, no field, not required, not bound,
Just listen to his heart and be deaf to all that's around,
It is good he should leave all he has found.
For he'll listen to his heart and his life he will know
And he'll know what there is and feel what he owes.

פתיחה: לבד

Opening: Alone

כְּצֵאתִי אֶת־הָעִיר, אֶפְרֹשׂ אֶת־כַּפַּי אֶל־ה׳.

שמות ט, כט

When I leave the city, I will spread my hands to the Lord.

Exodus 9:29

And another time [Rebbe Nahman] told us that in his youth he would perform hitbodedut in some forest or field, and when he would return from there the whole world seemed as if new in his eyes and it seemed as if it was a completely different world and the world didn't seem as it had previously at all.

Rebbe Natan of Breslov, *Ḥayei Moharan* 107

The Rebbe said that it is very good even to just sit in such a special room. The atmosphere itself is beneficial, even if you sit there and do nothing else. Even if you do not have a special room, you can still seclude yourself and converse with God.

The Rebbe also said that you can create your own special room under your prayer shawl. Just drape it over your eyes and converse with God as you desire. You can also seclude yourself with God in bed under the covers. This was the custom of King David, as it is written, "Each night I converse from my bed..." (Ps. 6:7).

Rebbe Nahman of Breslov, *Siḥot HaRan* 275

From days past and years ancient
Even before the prayers were established
The prayer book had not yet been written, the text not yet cast,
There was *hitbodedut*, a person's private prayer of the heart:
A person stands alone

Pouring out words
Before God.

Rebbe Nahman of Breslov
Who elevated *hitbodedut* to be a foundation of Divine service
Tried to precede the frame to the content.
As opposed to the awareness of one praying from a prayer book,
Who is focused on the content, on the number of words that
 need to be said,
Rebbe Nahman suggests we focus on the framework:
An hour a day, pick a place and stand before God.
What will happen there? What will you say?
Come and see.
The challenge is to show up. To allow life to reverberate within
 me and see what arises,
To open a regular channel of talking to God.
If in our set prayer the challenge is to give the words heart
In *hitbodedut* it's the opposite: the challenge is to give the
 heart words.

It is important to step out of known surroundings, worn-out
 terrain,
And create, as much as possible, a regularity of time and place.
A set time, an hour, or half-an-hour a day,
A place where I can be in intimate communication with my
 Creator,
Where I can truly open my heart.
In a special room, under a prayer shawl or beneath the covers
Or even amongst a crowd, under an invisible veil:
Hitbodedut.

צעד ראשון של התבודדות
The Initial Step of *Hitbodedut*

And every person should set for himself for this some time every day, to speak out his words before God in the language that he speaks, for in the language a person speaks it is easier to express his words well, and everything that is in his heart he should say before God with claims and explanations and words of appeasement and supplication, that he should merit to come close to Him, every person as he knows the pains of his heart and how far away he is from God. And the actual spiritual level of this action cannot be explained or estimated, for this is above everything and includes the entire service of God. For through this one can come to all the good in this world and the next. For one can achieve anything through praying and pleading. And all the great holy people only came to their high level through this action…. Happy is the one who merits to set for himself a special time of day every day for this, and the rest of the day he should be happy.

Rebbe Nahman of Breslov, *Likutei Eitzot – Hitbodedut*

- Where can we do *hitbodedut*?
  Outside of the city, away from the hustle and bustle and endless distractions.
  If our circumstances prevent us from going out into nature,
  It is important to choose a place where we can feel quiet, calm, relaxed.
  Perhaps on our porch, in our garden, or even in bed under the covers.

- How do we do *hitbodedut*?
  Standing,
  Sitting,
  Walking,
  Lying down,
  Whatever feels right.

- How do we begin?
  It is a good idea to begin with a few minutes of silence,
  To go quietly inside, to sense our body, our breath,
  To listen to the surrounding sounds,
  To notice what comes up inside of me.

- When we feel ready, we can begin speaking.
  As in any conversation, we begin by addressing our words.
  We don't mumble to ourselves, but rather call out with a specific name,
  The name of the One with whom we are speaking.
  The Master of the World has many names and titles,

Which can fit different types of conversations,
And so it is worthwhile to find the name that fits the moment.
Even if no specific name is preferred, it is important to choose one.

- We dedicate our initial words to thanks and praise,
  For all the kindness,
  For all the good that has come to us till this very day.
  We appreciate it and express our gratitude.
  I thank You for… It amazes me that…
  Afterward we can begin to request,
  To pour out our heart.
  I ask You to… I so want…
  We can also share with the Holy Blessed One,
  To make God a partner in what happened to us today, events large or small.
  I wanted You to know…

- When we feel that we have exhausted what we have to say, we end as we began – with words of thanks and praise. We can repeat the same things we said before, or mention something we remembered as we spoke. We can thank God for listening and for the very ability to do *hitbodedut*, to speak and to share.
  It is a good idea to pause for a few more moments in silence, in order to allow the words to be absorbed.

- It is also possible to do *hitbodedut* as part of a group. When we do so, it is a good idea to set times for each stage of *hitbodedut* and to appoint someone in the group to be responsible to announce when it's time to move from stage to stage. This will make it easier for everyone to give themselves over to talking, without feeling the need to check the time.

A summary of the above:

Sitting quietly
Addressing, choosing the right name to call
Giving thanks
Requesting
Sharing
Again, thanking
Concluding in silence.

תפילה בין העשבים
Praying in the Field

It is good and pleasing when going out to converse [lasuaḥ] in the field, for this conversation [siḥa] is prayer and pleading and passion for the Holy Blessed One. When every bush [siaḥ] of the field begins to return to life and grow, they all yearn to be included in prayer and meditation [siḥa].

Rebbe Nahman of Breslov, *Likutei Siḥot* 98

Know! When a person prays in the fields, all the flora enters into the prayer, helping him and strengthening his prayer. This is the reason prayer is called conversation [siḥa], the concept of "shrub [siaḥ] of the field" (Gen. 2:5). All the shrubs of the field empower and assist his prayer.

This is the concept of "And Isaac went to converse [lasuaḥ] in the field" (Gen. 24:63)– his prayer was with the help and power of the field. All the flora of the field empowered and assisted his prayer, on account of which prayer is called siḥa.

Rebbe Nahman of Breslov, *Likutei Moharan*, part 2, *torah* 11

When praying in the forest
In a field or a garden
Among the trees and the grass,
When we distance ourselves from civilization
Lower the volume,
We can hear the murmurings of the field
The song of the land
The prayer rising up from all of creation
To the Living God.
We are able to feel the power of growth hidden in the grasses
To be a mouth for their longings
To give words to their movements in the wind
To murmur the murmurs of their leaves
To become one with the trees of the forest.

- Going out to a field, amidst the grass,
  Quieting, listening to their whisper, to their silent movement,
  Imagining ourselves as the *sheliaḥ tzibur* for the blades of grass,
  Being a shofar for their praises,
  Listening to their appeal, their exchange.
  We give voice to what we hear.
  Whispers, movements, voices, words, supplications, thanks.
  We raise our voice ever so slightly.

- Now, with the same sensitivity, we listen to what is going on inside us.
  We let the movement of the grass beat through our prayers,
  We allow the voices to rise, the entreaties to grow, the desires to sprout.
  We allow our prayer to be like the prayer of the grass, raw and simple.
  We sound out what we hear,
  Imagining the words of the grass joining our conversation,
  The song of the Earth singing.
  We give them voice, and take our leave with quiet listening.

התבודדות מבקשת
Requesting in *Hitbodedut*

Rebbe Nahman said more on the topic of hitbodedut. The Rebbe, of blessed memory, avidly encouraged the regular practice of hitbodedut, speaking with God each and every day. He said: Even when one cannot speak at all, or says only a single thing – it is also very good! He also said: Even if a person can only say one thing, he should be resolute and say that thing over and over again, endlessly. And even if he spends many, many days saying nothing but this thing – that too is good! He should be strong and courageous, and continue to say that thing countless times until God takes pity on him and opens his mouth, enabling him to elaborate his words.

Rebbe Nahman of Breslov, *Likutei Moharan*, part 2, torah 96

Hitbodedut can be an opportunity to turn to God
With a plea, with an appeal.
To lay out before God our heart's desire, the needs of our life.
To request
Something in our soul now.
To pinpoint our desire
To refine a single prayer
To repeat it
Again and again
To make an opening for it
To plead for it in prayer.

- We sit in *hitbodedut*,
  Open with words of thanks and praise
  And move on to a request.
  We shouldn't get scattered with many different requests,
  But rather attempt to touch on just one desire,
  That suits us right now.

- We return to this request again and again,
  Pleading, attempting to create an opening for it,
  Maybe from here, maybe from there,
  Entreating, begging,
  Explaining –
  Why is this so important to me?
  Why do I deserve this?
  Why do I think this is good for me?

- And after the words,
  An enormous pain remains within,
  A deep feeling that can't be expressed in words,
  And so it is good at times to add a scream,
  To extract this pain,
  To bring it into our conversation.

A summary of the above:

An opening with thanks
A precise request
A repetition of the request
A scream (if it's fitting)

התבודדות משתפת
Hitbodedut: A Sharing

יֶעֱרַב נָא שִׂיחִי עָלֶיךָ כִּי נַפְשִׁי תַעֲרוֹג אֵלֶיךָ.

רבי יהודה החסיד, שיר הכבוד

May my words be pleasing to You, for my soul yearns for You.

Rabbi Yehuda HeHasid, *Shir HaKavod*

The Rebbe often spoke to us about conversing with God. Speak to God in order to understand your purpose in life. Think about yourself and beg God to help you find Him. Use whatever language you speak best, and argue with God, petitioning Him in every way. All these thoughts appear in the Rebbe's published works, but beyond this, he would frequently discuss this most important concept. For if you set aside a time each day to converse with God, you will surely be worthy of finding Him. You may do this for days and years, apparently without effect, but in the end you will reach your goal.

Rebbe Nahman of Breslov, *Sihot HaRan* 68

Beyond the requests, the pleas, the praise and the gratitude
Beyond the silence and the scream
Hitbodedut can simply be a conversation.
A conversation without the burden of a mission,
Rather a meeting of two.

Simple talk,
That seeks to share, to come close.
A conversation is by nature mutual
Demonstrating clearly the presence of two.
This shared *hitbodedut* opens a channel of conversation
    between myself and my Creator,
Inviting God to hear me, to turn to me.
Involving the Holy Blessed One in the stories of our lives
Transforms God into a partner.
Small, simple moments
Find meaning,
Are gathered into the infinite,
Engraved in eternity.

- We set a specific time in our day, and a place where we will do *hitbodedut*, just as we'd set a meeting. We can show up with a cup of coffee or tea in hand, sit down comfortably. We open ourselves to the presence of the Holy Blessed One around us and within us.

- Opening the conversation, with simple language, we share with God moments and thoughts from the day that has passed. Talk with no specific purpose, not focused on needs or requests. We shouldn't worry about being too banal or trite. Every word that arises has a place and is a part of the sharing.

- We feel the merit we have, to stand facing the Creator of the World, who takes interest in us. We give thanks for the merit we have to share our lives with God.

Drawing Out Prayers לדלות תפילות

Therefore great is peace and love between Israel, as it is written, "You should love your friend as yourself," and Rabbi Akiva said this is a great rule in the Torah. For through the love between one another, through this they become included in one another and shine to each other and receive from each other.

Rebbe Natan of Breslov, *Likutei Halakhot, Oraḥ Ḥayim, Birkhot HaRe'iya* 1

The inner movement of prayer is the search for inner will
Each one of us is like a ray of infinite will
But this desire is clothed in many forms, concealed in
 hiddenness.
I must penetrate the deepest point of prayer within me
The innermost, painful point burning within
A refined point, lacking all outer shells and covers.
Prisoners cannot free themselves from jail
Sometimes, in order to find our innermost will,
We need the assistance of another
A good friend can help us find our prayer
To be like a water carrier
Drawing our prayer from the depths
And like a midwife, breaking the waters of our prayers.

- We sit together as a pair, our bodies facing one another, listening. Our eyes looking, attentive. One shares a prayer that they have been carrying lately, a request they have, an inner desire.

- The listener attempts to clarify with the one asking their deepest desire, helping them birth a most precise prayer.

    For example:
    - I want to have a lot of money.
    - Why? What would you do with the money?
    - I would found a non-profit organization for professional guidance/I would build a big house/I would retire.
    - So that what will happen?
    - I will make a difference in the world/I'll make my mother happy/I'll be able to relax.
    - And then what?
    - ...

- The exact same request is bound to have a completely different meaning, depending on who's asking. After three such questions whose purpose is to arrive to the essence of the request, the prayer will be revealed and will rise from its source.

- After the prayer is born, each one can find a place to pray and then turn to God.

המתפלל על חברו
One Who Prays for a Friend

Anyone who asks for compassion [from Heaven] on behalf of another

And he requires the same thing

He is answered first.

As it is written: "And the Lord changed the fortune of Job

When he prayed for his friends" (Job 42:10).

Bava Kamma 92a

Before one sets his prayer in the synagogue from the passage of the Binding [of Isaac] and on, one must accept on himself the commandment of "And love your friend as yourself," and have in mind to love every one of the Jewish people as himself.... And specifically loving the friends who learn Torah together, every one of them should include himself as if he were one of his friends' limbs, especially if a person has knowledge and awareness to know and recognize his friend on the level of soul. And if one of the friends is in trouble, they all should feel a part of his pain or sickness, or trouble with his children, God forbid. And they should pray for him, and similarly in all of one's prayers and needs and matters, he should include his friend with him.

Rabbi Hayim Vital, *Shaar HaKavanot, Drushei Birkat HaShaḥar*

It is often very difficult for us to pray for ourselves with all of our might

We get all complicated:

I'm not comfortable asking, I don't really deserve it, I can deal with it on my own.

There is something freeing about praying for another:

It's not me – it's my friend

I'm not doing this for myself.

And this allows me to put all my strength into the prayer.

By asking my friend to pray for me, I release my grip on the problem,

And give it over to my friend.

Somebody else is carrying my baggage

Relieving me of the weight for a moment.

I'm not alone.

When I pray for a friend, I am essentially expressing my readiness to take their troubles from them,

To take responsibility for them for a while, to deal with things for them.

I reach out a hand,

And pray.

Recipe for praying with a friend or *ḥavruta*

- Sitting together in a comfortable, quiet place, we decide who will be first to share and who will take the role of the listener; later we will switch.

- The one speaking thinks of a hardship, problem, or request they'd like to ask their friend to pray for on their behalf. They share with their friend in detail. (They can also ask their friend to help them draw out the prayer as was demonstrated on the previous page.)

- The listener should check with the friend that all that was said was heard. Obviously, this is not the place for critique or for offering advice, but rather solely for listening. To summarize the conversation, write down the request together.

- Switch roles and the one who previously listened, now becomes the speaker, and the one who spoke, now listens.

- After this mutual sharing, the time has come for prayer. Each one prays for the desire heard from the other. Find a place to pray. We may stay close to our friend or we may spread out. We choose a specific name of God to whom we will turn, tell God of our friend's request, and ask for salvation in our own words. It is a good idea to note the name of our friend's father and mother. We can try to expand the prayer, to repeat it, to explain it, to plead it, to knock on the Heavenly door for them. To cry out to God about it from the depths of our heart, for our friend.

בשיחה מתמדת

In Constant Conversation

Master of the World,
Who listens to the voice of our prayers
And our words and our pleas,
Teach me how to bring You new and beautiful words.
And You know, my father in Heaven, that all my hope
And all of my anticipation
Is on the prayer and the supplications and the cries and the screams to You.
But how do I find new words as I need each and every day
In such a manner that I will merit to please You truly?
Send me the spirit of Your holiness.
At every moment, place new, pleasant and beautiful words
With which I can please You.
You Who are filled with compassion, Who has mercy on the poor,
Who thinks of perfecting me even now,
Open Your mouth to a mute like me and show me what I may say.

Give me understanding of what I should
   ask.
"My God, open my lips and my mouth
   will speak Your praise."
Have compassion on me and help me
   so that I will engage in a great deal of
   conversation that is prayer
Between myself and my Maker
Every day of my life.
Send me new, holy, and beautiful words at
   all times.
Give me new words.

Likutei Tefillot, part 1, prayer 118

One Who Will Pray

Yitzhak Lamdan

Indeed it happens even these days
Suddenly one will stand and pray,
And the man is not in a prayer shawl wrapped –
With his tie tied and his shoes polished,
He bows not in a temple,
    or in a house of prayer –
In the middle of the city next to the tram,
While awaiting traincar number this or that
He'll stand up and pray to one he feels:
Is there.

פתיחה: הֱיֵה בעל תפילה!
Opening: Be a Master of Prayer!

The soul is always praying. Indeed, it [constantly] flies up and embraces its beloved without any pause at all?... Prayer is likened to a rose that opens its beautiful leaves for the dew or before the rays of sun that appear on it with light, and therefore "if only a person would pray throughout the entire day" (Berakhot 21a).

Rabbi Avraham Yitzhak HaKohen Kook, *Olat Re'iya, Inyenei Tefilla*, The Constant Prayer of the Soul, 2

A person stands and prays and contemplates in his heart, and the Holy Blessed One is close and hears his prayer, as it is said: "The one Who hears prayers, to You all flesh comes" (Ps. 65).

Deuteronomy Rabba, *Parashat Vaethanan, parasha bet*

When creating the world, the Creator agreed to contract.
The Infinite donned limitation, finiteness,
The material world.
And this is what we have.
In this world walk those who pray,
Bending an ear, listening, opening an eye,
They hear, see, and meet the infinite within the finite,
They listen to the longings, to the yearnings,
To the heart inside everything.
Everything desires prayer,
Everything is expecting,
Waiting for some warm words that will redeem them from their loneliness, from their finiteness, from their sadness.
The movement of the waves, of trees in the wind, is like the movement of swaying in prayer:
A movement of infinite longing.
The words of prayer are a bridge of words over the chasm of distance and separation.
The Infinite, hidden in what is,
Expecting someone to come and to reveal what is inside,
The movement,
The longing, the hope, the desires, and the yearnings.
And you,
Go on your way,
Be attentive to the voice of constant prayer
Pulsating through all the dimensions of life,
Prayer seeking connection, asking for contact and presence.
Collect the prayers that are out there on their own,
With no prayer leader, no *sheliaḥ tzibur*,
Be a master of prayer.

ההסתכלת היום אל השמים?
Have You Looked at the Skies Today?

One time when there was a fair in Breslov, and [a merchant and Hasid of Rebbe Nahman's] ran quickly to the market to buy and sell. He [Rebbe Nahman] said to him: "Did you look at the sky today?"

And he said: "No!"

He called him to the window

And he said to him: "What do you see?"

He said: "I see wagons and horses and people running back and forth."

He said to him:

"Fifty years from now there will be a completely different fair; other horses and other wagons and people.

I will not be here, nor will you.

So today I ask you:

Do you not even have time to look at the sky?"

Rebbe Avraham of Tultchin, *Kokhavei Or*, *Anshei Moharan*, paragraph 5

We walk through this world with a quick step
On a noisy road
On a crowded street
We move forward
Our thoughts racing inside
And sometimes out of nowhere, our head suddenly looks above
Sees a piece of sky
A ray of light
A cloud
And remembers
There are skies above me
For a brief moment we are pulled out of life's race, from the confusion, from the futility.
The skies stretch above us from horizon to horizon
Reminding us of God's infiniteness
When something is stuck
When there is no way out
We don't know what to do
We don't know what to say
We can, for just a moment
Turn our eyes upward
Look to the skies, and discover the Heavens.

Hints

רמזים

Each day has in it thought, word, and deed. The Holy One, blessed be He, contracts His Godliness ad infinitum, to the center point of the material world [on which man] stands. He arranges for him thought, word, and deed according to the particular day, and the particular person, and the particular place. And He enclothes hints for him in his thought, word, and deed that He arranges for him, in order to bring him closer to serving Him. Therefore, a person has to think deeply about this, and to expand his understanding – to understand what the particular hints are that are enclothed in the thought, word, and deed of this day that the Holy One has arranged for him, whether in physical labor or business activity. And in all this that the Holy One arranges for him each day, he has to deepen and expand his thoughts so as to understand the hints of the Holy One.

Rebbe Nahman of Breslov, *Litkuei Moharan*, part 1, torah 54

From the Priestly Blessing,
From the reading of the Torah,
From the "Amen" that we answered after the *sheliaḥ tzibur*,
From the *hitbodedut* and the prayer
We move on to our daily routine.

We carry with us the habit of listening,
Of seeking an answer,
And we carry this beyond to what is happening
To us and around us,
Throughout the day.

This has a little bit of what Rabbi Yoḥanan taught: "If only a person would pray all day long" (Berakhot 21a).
Prayer is continuous,
Emerging,
Alive and whispering around us.
All that happens is full of hints
And everything that happens to me – hearkens to me.
[Of course, we don't have to exaggerate.
Otherwise we'll find ourselves overwhelmed.
Focused on interpreting, rather than living, our lives.]

- Throughout the day, as the desire comes, or an inner feeling arises,
  We can say thank you for a hint that was understood.
  Or we can pray to understand something that happened:
  God, I don't understand,
  What do You mean by this?
  Can You make it clear to me, please?

- We won't always get an answer,
  But it's important that we attempt to be in dialogue with reality,
  To draw words from it,
  To transform life into a constant conversation.

כתיבת תפילות
Writing Prayers

Rabbi Pedat in the name of Rabbi Yaakov ben Idi said: Rabbi Eliezer would pray three prayers [a day]. And after his prayer what did he say? May it be Your will, my God and the God of my forefathers, that the hatred of us should not come into the heart of any man, nor the hatred of another into our heart, and jealousy of us should not enter the heart of a person, nor the jealousy of another into our heart, and let Your Torah be our work all the days of our lives and let our words be supplications before You. Rabbi Ḥiyya bar Abba added: And focus our heart to be in awe of Your name, and distance from us all that You hate, and bring us close to all that You love, act charitably with us for the sake of Your name. The study house of Rabbi Yannai said: One who awakes from sleep should say: Blessed are You God who gives life to the dead. My Master, I have sinned to You. Let it be Your will my God that You should give me a good heart, a good portion, a good friend, a good eye, a good soul, a humble soul, and a low spirit.

Y. Berakhot 7:2

And many times he would speak before God words of supplication and request from his heart and there would come in his words beautiful claims and set and upright prayers, and they were pleasing to him and he would write them to himself to remember so that he should be regular in praying those prayers afterward as well, and he was also regular in speaking to God very many, many times, and all of his prayers were that he should merit to come close to God and he had much to say to God about this.

Rebbe Natan of Breslov, *Shivḥei HaRan*, 11

One way we can make prayer part of our day-to-day life
And give it space to enter into different parts of our lives
Is by writing our own prayers.
A prayer for livelihood, a prayer to find a spouse, a prayer for peace in our homes, a prayer about pollution and about the car that once again broke down. A prayer about our connection with our neighbors, a prayer in anticipation of a birth, or a prayer before setting out on a journey.

Writing a prayer gives voice to what is going on inside of me,
Transforming a vague desire into something clear.
The writing gives substance and power to our desire,
Revealing and exposing its depth.
A prayer I have written leaves me and can touch others for whom my prayer –
Is theirs.
And the writing makes it possible for me to say the prayer again and again,
To return to the words that I formed and to find precision, from the innermost place.

A few initial pieces of advice when trying to write a prayer:

- It's a good idea to have a dedicated journal, or a specific file on the computer, and to choose a quiet time and place. Close the door, or go out to a quiet spot in nature, and silence any distractions like a cellphone.

- The name that we choose to address in our prayer can be a key for the words that will follow – we can let it guide us.

- We may choose to follow the traditional form of a known prayer, for example praise, request, and thanksgiving, or to pave a new path altogether.

- It's good to pay attention in what voice we choose to speak our prayer – first person singular, plural, or omniscient.

- After our first writing it's a good idea to read what we've written out loud. Hearing the sound of the words can help us sharpen and clarify our words.

In Closing, a Prayer

תפילה לסיום

Our God in Heaven
God, May You be blessed, the Holy Blessed One, the Doer of
    Great Deeds, the Knower of Mysteries
The One I Know Not
Please
    Please God
I'm begging of You,
Hearer of Prayers
Even these fragmented pieces that aren't even really shaped
Or polished
Please God
Please You, yes, You Master of mercy, Who hears prayers and
    listens to cries
Who is reconciled by our tears and who fashions our hearts
In Your great mercy
Make delicacies of the recipes presented here
That they should make an opening like the tiny hole of a
    needle
In the hearts of Your children, Israel
Who are very eager and want
To pray before You, God, to pray
And don't always know how to, so here is an attempt to guide,
    to direct, But the main thing is that
An opening like the tiny hole of a needle should open
And the shell of the heart should crack
So a prayer can slip out
Please.

Copyright list

Excerpts from *Rebbe Nachman's Wisdom* (*Sichot HaRan and Shevachey HaRan*), by Rabbi Natan of Nemirov. Translated and annotated by Rabbi Aryeh Kaplan. Edited by Rabbi Zvi Aryeh Rosenfeld (Jerusalem: Breslov Research Institute), 1973.

Excerpts from *The Fiftieth Gate: Likutey Tefilot, Reb Noson's Prayers*, translated by Yaacov Dovid Shulman (Jerusalem: Breslov Research Institute), 1993.

Excerpts from *Tzaddik: A Portrait of Rabbi Nachman*, translated by Avraham Greenbaum (Jerusalem: Breslov Research Institute), 1987.

Excerpts from *Likutey Moharan*, by Nachman of Breslov. Translated by Simcha Bergman and Moshe Mykoff (Jerusalem: Breslov Research Institute), 1986–2012.

© All rights reserved to the Breslov Research Institute

"Then my soul will say..." / Pinhas Sadeh
© All rights reserved to the author and ACUM – The Society of Authors, Composers, and Music Publishers in Israel

"In the Beginning" / Rivka Miriam
© All rights reserved to the author and ACUM

"Longing" / Miriam Barukh Halfi
© All rights reserved to the author and ACUM

"Contact" / Sivan Har Shefi
© All rights reserved to the author

"You are the Voice" / Michal Govrin
© All rights reserved to the author and ACUM

"Everyone Needs" / Chana Friedman Uhlman
© All rights reserved to the author

Ancient Song / Zelda
© All rights reserved to the author and ACUM

"In My Descent" / Sivan Har Shefi
From *Tehilim LeYom Ra'ash* (Tel Aviv: Hakibbutz Hameuchad – Sifriat Poalim), 2010, p. 59 [Hebrew].
© All rights reserved to the author and the publisher

"Sought" / Admiel Kosman
© All rights reserved to the author and ACUM

"Good for a Man" / Zalman Shazar
© All rights reserved to the author and the Zalman Shazar Center

"One Who Will Pray" / Yitzhak Lamdan
From *Kol Shirei Yitzhak Lamdan* (Jerusalem: Bialik Institute), 1973, p. 100 [Hebrew].
© All rights reserved to the author and the publisher

We thank all of the artists who have given permission for their work to appear in this book. We have made every effort to locate the copyright holders of all material from external sources. We apologize for any errors or omissions in copyright acknowledgements and permissions referenced in this book and would be grateful to be notified of any corrections or permissions that should be incorporated in future reprints or editions.

About the Author

Rabbi Dov Singer, a leader of the modern Israeli revival of Hassidut, heads the innovative Makor Chaim Yeshiva, founded by Rabbi Adin Steinsaltz. Influenced by the Zohar, Rebbe Nachman of Breslov, and other Hassidic thinkers, Rabbi Singer's unique educational approach is predicated on the development of religious and emotional intelligence. He leads workshops on prayer throughout Israel and the United States, and has also established the Study Center for Renewal, an adult spiritual outreach program, and *Lifnai VeLifnim*, an educators' training program. Rabbi Singer lives in Israel with his wife and ten children.

The fonts used in this book are from the Arno Koren family

Maggid Books
*The best of contemporary Jewish thought from
Koren Publishers Jerusalem Ltd.*